The Prayer Adventure

Cliff Tadema

Westview Publishing
Mount Vernon WA

© Cliff Tadema 2021. The Prayer Adventure. All rights reserved.

All scripture quotations are taken from the HOLY BIBLE: New Living Translation 1996, 2004, 2015 TYNDALE HOUSE FOUNDATION or ENGLISH STANDARD VERSION © 2012, 2016 as taken from Logos Bible Software, Faithlife Corporation. Licensed use. Atlas copyright © 2016 Mapbox. All rights reserved.

Permission to copy or use portions of this text may be granted by contacting the author in writing and receiving written expressed permission. Use without permission is prohibited.

ISBN: 978-0-9863258-5-4
Printed in the United States of America through Westview Publishing.

Jacqueline Rae, Editor
Jaycee Day, Cover Design

Contents

5	Introduction
15	Day 1: Communicating for Relationship
20	Day 2: Intimacy with God Impacts Others
26	Day 3: Your Purpose in Communicating with God
32	Day 4: Communication with God
38	Day 5: The Power in a God Relationship
44	Day 6: God and My Ups and Downs
50	Day 7: The Pathway to Help from God
56	Day 8: Setting the Stage
62	Day 9: Affirming the Positions
67	Day 10: Presenting Requests
73	Day 11: Clearing the Static
79	Day 12: Establishing Direction
85	Day 13: Connecting the Power
90	Day 14: Reflecting on the Manual
96	Day 15: Telling the Truth
102	Day 16: Protecting the Heart
107	Day 17: Praying in Peace
112	Day 18: Praying with Faith
118	Day 19: Salvation and Prayer
124	Day 20: Wielding a Sword
130	Day 21: Armor Reflection

135	Day 22: The Impact of Prayerlessness
141	Day 23: The Roadblock of Unconfessed Sin
147	Day 24: Compelling Confessions
153	Day 25: Roadblock of Broken Relationships
159	Day 26: The Roadblock of Selfishness
165	Day 27: The Value of Faithful Prayers
171	Day 28: Restful Prayers
176	Day 29: Is it His Will?
182	Day 30: Waiting Patiently
188	Day 31: Testing Your Faith
194	Day 32: The Big Picture
200	Day 33: Is Anything In Between?
206	Day 34: …Yet I Will Rejoice
212	Day 35: Getting Better Results
218	Day 36: Persistence Pays
224	Day 37: All Occasions
230	Day 38: Staying Aligned
236	Day 39: Being Proactive
242	Day 40: Staying Alert
248	Bonus Day – One: United in Prayer
254	Bonus Day – Two: Don't Give Up!
260	The Key is Prayer
261	S O A P S

Introduction

Prayer works! It's not a question. It is a fact. One independent study after another and one blind test after another concludes that prayer works. It even works for those that don't know they are being prayed for! In blind tests, people who were prayed for fared better, healed faster, and remained more positive than those who were intentionally not being prayed for. Prayer does in fact, work.

As a pastor, I have found one common ingredient, one secret weapon in churches that experience healthy growth. That secret weapon is prayer. It won't always be obvious, and I've never seen it to be the majority of the people. But the people who are praying in those settings take it seriously and understand that God does something in the spiritual realm when we pray that we cannot understand but we do eventually see.

If prayer is effective, then why don't more people pray and pray effectively? The major reason is that people don't or won't take the time and initiative to make it a habit; to purposefully make it a lifestyle. And that's what The Prayer Adventure is all about. The Prayer Adventure provides a way for you to establish and create the healthy habit of prayer and in the process for you to see how God will use it to change you for your good and God's glory.

Physical exercise is good for you. Evidence for the value of physical exercise in our lives is overwhelming. Physical exercise improves your health, makes you feel better, perform more efficiently, have more confidence, and live longer. And yet many of us have a difficult time establishing a routine and/or lifestyle that promotes exercise on a regular basis. Part of this has to do with the ease or difficulty we find in establishing new habits. Research tells us that it takes a minimum of 21 days to establish a habit.

The Value of a Number

I'm enamored with God's word. It captivates me, intrigues me, motivates me, and gives me a reason for living. The more I come to know about it the more I realize I don't know. As an example, it has always fascinated me how God has chosen to use some numbers. I don't want to get off on what's known as numerology here but there is a number that's worth our attention as we prepare to take this journey together. It's fascinating how God has used it and it has value for us here.

The number 40 is one of those fascinating numbers. Moses was in the desert for 40 years before God used him to free the Israelites from the Egyptians. Moses was also on the mountain for 40 days experiencing God in a life changing way. Noah saw rain come down in torrents for 40 days and it changed the known world. Jesus spent 40 days in the desert right after his baptism and prior to starting his ministry. In every 40-day instance in the Bible the people who went through it were dramatically affected by God for their good and His glory. And that's my prayer for you!

Perhaps because of this many people have used the 40-day idea to establish a new normal. Several authors have written 40-day prayer challenges and they're just dandy. But I needed one for me and people like me. One that is all inclusive and keeps me on track. And I wanted one that was 40 days plus two. The reason: If it takes a minimum of 21 days to make a habit then I need at least double that!

Moses ended up going up the mountain twice for 40 days. And you might find it necessary to go over The Prayer Adventure more than one time as well. I would encourage you to do it as often as necessary until it becomes part of who you are!

The Prayer Goal

Moses' purpose in going up that mountain for 40 days, twice, was to get to know God and His will. He wanted to lead and live the way God wanted him to. We have the same goal with The Prayer Adventure. As you joyfully work your way through it, my prayer is that God will show you more and more what His will is for you and your life. And while you are doing it, keep doing it with others. God loves it when we grow together!

Jesus said to his disciples, which includes his followers today, in *John 14:12-14, Whatever you ask in my name, this I will do, that the Father may be glorified in the Son.* *14 If you ask me anything in my name, I will do it.* This does not mean that all we have to do is conclude any prayer we choose to make with, "In Jesus name, Amen!" Nope – when I first read this scripture, I thought it was my winning lottery ticket! So, I tried it... and it didn't work. And then I found out that what Jesus meant is that if we are praying HIS WILL, meaning God's will for us and the circumstances we are praying for *then* He will do it! That makes understanding and knowing His will to be critical for the content and success of our prayers.

The goal of The Prayer Adventure isn't to find out how to get what you want. If that was your goal, I'm sorry to disappoint you. The goal here is greater than that. It's to find out what God wants, what God wills and to learn to pray about that!

Often, I start my prayers by praying scripture and then I'll find myself asking God what else to pray about. Other times I have a laundry list of things I want to get through and make God aware of. As I wait, God brings to my mind a person, a problem or one of His promises, and off we go. There is a real comfort and certainty in praying God's will. By the time you conclude The Prayer Adventure, you'll have a better idea of what that is for you!

The Place of Prayer

Where you pray is far less important than that you pray. But it is helpful to establish your preferred prayer "place." At one of the places we lived, I was able to build, what I called, "My worship spot." It was a place in the woods, under a canopy that looked over a little creek. I loved to pray and worship God there. Where we live now it's more difficult to find a place that offers some privacy and sets an appropriate ambiance. So, I move around a bit and sometimes just go for a drive for that alone time with God.

The attitude we pray with establishes our mental "place of prayer." This is important because it does make a difference to God. God wants us to be humble when we approach Him, and He wants us to turn away from doing wrong. This is made clear in, 2 Chronicles 7:14, which says:

"If my people who are called by my name humble themselves and pray and seek my face and turn from their wicked ways, then I will hear from heaven and will forgive their sin and heal their land."

Some time ago, my wife, Caryn, and I were talking about prayer and hearing from God. She said that she seemed to have hit a wall where she wasn't hearing from Him. It had become increasingly frustrating to her. I asked if she was consistently praying. She assured me she was and talked about the many things she was consistently praying about. I said, "The only thing I can think of is to keep on keeping on and to ask God why He isn't speaking to you more clearly."

Caryn's preferred place of prayer is often her car. For some reason she senses God's presence there and God has often spoken to her very clearly in her car. The next day, she was driving and praying. (When you're praying and driving it's okay to pray with your eyes open). She prayed, in frustration, "Lord why am I not hearing You and why aren't You speaking to me? I'm praying for these things but don't sense You!"

Suddenly she heard, in her mind, the Holy Spirit say, "Do you want to hear me? Quit praying for a life where I'm not necessary." She pulled over to the side of the road and began to weep as she remembered the content of her prayers over the past weeks. One of the big misconceptions about prayer is that we are supposed to bring our laundry list of needs and wants and present it to God for Him to fulfill as a to-do list.

When Caryn shared her experience with me later that evening, I was convicted myself. How often is the content of my prayers all about God providing things so that I don't have to depend on Him? Concentrating on doing our best to find out His will and praying for it, keeps us from selfish self-centered prayers. The great value in prayer is more about getting to know God and His character better than it is about informing God about our needs and wants with the expectation that He meets them.

Make A Record

The Prayer Adventure is designed as a journal. This is so you can record what God says and does over the next 40 plus days of your prayer adventure. Too often we pray for something and then forget about it. Then, when God does answer, we don't give Him glory because we've forgotten about it. **So, document your prayers and God's answers.**

This journal will prove of the greatest value to you and your prayer life if you take the time to actually write out the answers to the questions asked, each day. In addition, if you take the journaling part of it seriously, you will begin to hear from God more clearly and you'll come to know His voice.

As you journal, you might wonder, "Am I really hearing God or am I just making this up?" Or "What if this isn't from God but it's actually from the devil or some evil being? How do I know the difference?"

The answer is pretty simple and should encourage you to be willing to experiment with hearing God more freely. The Holy Spirit never contradicts himself. What that means is that He would never impress something on your mind or speak it to you in any way, including visions, words, impressions etc. that are not aligned with what He makes clear in His word, (The Bible).

Often people have asked me if what they heard and wrote was from God or if they just made it up. My answer is always the same. I ask a couple of questions:

> Does it line up with the Bible as truth from God?
> Is it an accurate reflection of God's character?

If the answer to those questions is, "yes." Then it doesn't matter if it was from the Holy Spirit or if they made it up. It's God's truth in either case. Usually, it's clear rather quickly if it's from God, from the person, or from our enemy.

Make A Commitment

Make a commitment to the process for the next 40 days plus. Nothing good and sustainable comes without a commitment. And it's best if the commitment can be made with partners. Get a group to go through the 40 days together. At the minimum do it with a partner so that you can encourage each other, support each other, and share with each other.

When we commit as a team, we get to share the victories and God's answers with others. One of the most encouraging aspects of The Prayer Adventure will be to hear about the different ways that God answers prayers and to share in the miracles that He will do.

A commitment like this will require a willingness to make some changes. It may mean changing your schedule by getting up earlier than you have. It could mean giving up a television show so you can repurpose the time for your prayer adventure. But the changes and the effort will be so very worth it. Here are the things you should commit to:

1. I will work through the Prayer Journal daily.
2. I will write down my requests and His answers.
3. I will pray daily, asking God to show me His will.
4. I will share the journey with others.
5. I will pray for God to do the miraculous for His glory.

X_____
Sign your name and write date.

Throughout the 40 plus days you may have different prayer requests that you will write down. But there may also be some major prayer requests that you would like to see God answer over the next 40 days. Write those prayer requests below. It's okay if they seem impossible. We serve a God who makes the impossible possible. Write them down so you remember to pray for them throughout the 40 days and so it will be clear when God answers them.

My Miracle Prayer List

1. _____

2. _____

3. _____

4. _____

5. _____

6. _____

7. _____

If you have more than seven, write them in any open spaces.

~~~~~~~~~~

I've been thinking about you a lot. With each paragraph written and each day of devotionals I thought about you. And as I pictured you, I started praying for you. And I kept on praying for you as I wrote each day and thought through the questions that would best give you insights into our amazing God. I thought about what your life might be like and what you might be experiencing. So, I prayed that the Holy Spirit would move powerfully in your life. I pray that He will use what is written in here and what he speaks to you through it to challenge, change, encourage and inspire you.

When God speaks to you in amazing ways. When He gives you insights that you know are not your own. And when He answers your prayers miraculously and spectacularly, I hope and pray that you will remember to share those victories, not just with others, but with me as well.

There were several times in the writing of this that I wanted to quit. After all, there are more prolific and far better authors who have written on the subject. But my wife, Caryn, reminded me of you. The people who could be changed by it. She encouraged me to keep thinking and praying for you.

So, we have prayed for you, and as I visualized the different people God would allow to have this journal, I asked Him how I could best pray for them. He led me to this prayer in His Word. Caryn and I are praying it for you. It comes from Colossians 1:9-14.

[9] And so, from the day we heard, we have not ceased to pray for you, asking that you may be filled with the knowledge of his will in all spiritual wisdom and understanding, [10] so as to walk in a manner worthy of the Lord, fully pleasing to him: bearing fruit in every good work and increasing in the knowledge of God; [11] being strengthened with all power, according to his glorious might, for all endurance and patience with joy; [12] giving thanks to the Father, who has qualified you to share in the inheritance of the saints in light.

Day 1

Communicating for Relationship

Pray: "Lord, speak to me through your Word and my prayers."

2 Samuel 7:18-29 (Excerpts)

Then King David went in and sat before the LORD and said, "Who am I, O Lord GOD, and what is my house, that you have brought me thus far? [19] And yet this was a small thing in your eyes, O Lord GOD. You have spoken also of your servant's house for a great while to come, and this is instruction for mankind, O Lord GOD! [20] And what more can David say to you? For you know your servant, O Lord GOD! [21] Because of your promise, and according to your own heart, you have brought about all this greatness, to make your servant know it. [22] Therefore you are great, O LORD God. For there is none like you, and there is no God besides you, according to all that we have heard with our ears. … [25] And now, O LORD God, confirm forever the word that you have spoken concerning your servant and concerning his house, and do as you have spoken. [26] And your name will be magnified forever, saying, 'The LORD of hosts is God over Israel,' and the house of your servant David will be established before you. [27] For you, O LORD of hosts, the God of Israel, have made this revelation to your servant, saying, 'I will build you a house.' Therefore, your servant has found courage to pray this prayer to you. [28] And now, O Lord GOD, you are God, and your words are true, and you have promised this good thing to your servant. [29] Now therefore may it please you to bless the house of your servant, so that it may continue forever before you. For you, O Lord GOD, have spoken, and with your blessing shall the house of your servant be blessed forever."

Communicating for Relationship

David knew the way to communicate with God is through dialogue. In verse 18 when it says that David "sat" it means that he remained; he spent a lengthy amount of time with God.

In verse 20 David acknowledged that God knows him already. God knows all there is to know about David and yet David still found importance in sitting and communicating with Him. It isn't that there is new information for David to share but that intimacy with God is gained through time spent with Him.

In spending time with God, David also demonstrated knowledge of God's heart. In verse 21; *For Your word's sake, and according to Your own heart, You have done all these great things, to make Your servant know them.*

He is thankful for what God has done in his life and who God is. David understands his valued role in the relationship... he states that he is God's 'servant'.

We can have an intimate relationship with the Lord. He has made it possible through Christ! God has designed us uniquely and wants a relationship with us that reflects that uniqueness. Your relationship with God shouldn't look like someone else's; it is a one-of-a-kind relationship, and it begins and is built on your communication with God.

Allow time today to remain in God. Sit and talk to Him. Get past your typical requests and daily prayers until you enter the deepest part of your thoughts to share with Him.

Prayer:

Lord, I'd like the kind of intimacy that David shared with you but unique to the way you made me. Please be my best friend and let the time we share together reflect that. I want to continually grow in my relationship with You. I'm asking you to do miraculous things in my life as I serve You. Show me the miracles You would like me to pray for and I'll write them down so that when You cause them to happen, I won't forget to praise you. Let me pray daringly for You and Your Kingdom and for me and my role in it. Start a new work in me today. In Jesus name, Amen.

Continue writing your prayer here:

Day 1: Communicating for Relationship

1. Write down some of the miracles you are boldly asking God for:

2. What do your times of sitting, or remaining, with God look like?

3. Ask God how can you improve your intimacy with Him... and then write down the answer:

Day 1: JOURNAL

Take a few moments to stop and LISTEN to the Lord; then write down what you sense He is telling you. Is He giving you words of encouragement for yourself that you should note? Is He asking you to encourage or support someone in particular? Is He showing you an adjustment you need to make in your life? Have you seen answered prayers? Write these things down so you create a record of God's goodness to you.

Day 2

Intimacy with God Impacts Others

Pray: "Lord, I accept your assignments for me, let them bless You."

Daniel 6 - Excerpts

Then this Daniel became distinguished above all the other high officials and satraps, because an excellent spirit was in him. And the king planned to set him over the whole kingdom. ⁴ Then the high officials and the satraps sought to find a ground for complaint against Daniel with regard to the kingdom, but they could find no ground for complaint or any fault, because he was faithful, and no error or fault was found in him. ⁵ Then these men said, "We shall not find any ground for complaint against this Daniel unless we find it in connection with the law of his God." ... ⁷ All the high officials of the kingdom, the prefects and the satraps, the counselors and the governors are agreed that the king should establish an ordinance and enforce an injunction, that whoever makes petition to any god or man for thirty days, except to you, O king, shall be cast into the den of lions. ... ⁹ Therefore King Darius signed the document and injunction. ¹⁰ When Daniel knew that the document had been signed, he went to his house where he had windows in his upper chamber open toward Jerusalem. He got down on his knees three times a day and prayed and gave thanks before his God, as he had done previously... ¹⁶ Then the king commanded, and Daniel was brought and cast into the den of lions. The king declared to Daniel, "May your God, whom you serve continually, deliver you!" ...

[19] Then, at break of day, the king arose and went in haste to the den of lions... The king declared to Daniel, "O Daniel, servant of the living God, has your God, whom you serve continually, been able to deliver you from the lions?" [21] Then Daniel said to the king, "O king, live forever! [22] My God sent his angel and shut the lions' mouths, and they have not harmed me, because I was found blameless before him; and also before you, O king, I have done no harm." [23] Then the king was exceedingly glad, and commanded that Daniel be taken up out of the den. So, Daniel was taken up out of the den, and no kind of harm was found on him, because he had trusted in his God.

Day 2: Intimacy with God Impacts Others

"I make a decree that in every dominion of my kingdom men must tremble and fear before the God of Daniel. For He is the living God, and steadfast forever; His kingdom is the one which shall not be destroyed, and His dominion shall endure to the end." Daniel 6:26

After Daniel was spared from the lion's den, King Darius believed in the power of Daniel's God and made this decree. Darius recognized not only who God is but also what God is capable of; *He delivers and rescues, and He works signs and wonders in heaven and on earth, who has delivered Daniel from the power of the lions. Daniel 6:27*

Daniel's intimacy in his relationship with God impacted his culture and those around him. It was scary at first and not what 'everyone' was doing. He was persecuted for his prayers and thrown into a den of lions. That's not exactly blending in with the crowd!

Ultimately his confidence in his relationship with God led to this decree and people believing in the true God. Daniels's confidence in God was built upon his constant communication with God. Communication led to certainty which led to conviction which led to confidence and trust in God. Daniel trusted God regardless of the outcome to him.

Daniel's intimacy in his relationship with God also gave a foundation for him to draw on in a time that would normally bring fear and doubt. *Daniel 6:10,11* shows that he spent time with God and that was his first priority. He was certain, even in the face of lions. Where and how do you get your time with the Lord?

Intimacy with God leads to amazing things, but it doesn't happen overnight. Like Daniel it takes time to pursue, worship, and prayer to build an uncompromising foundation.

Prayer:
Lord, I know that you are the living God, and your Kingdom won't be destroyed. Thank you for delivering and rescuing me. Please increase my faith that I might have a solid foundation built on you. Show me ways that my intimacy with You might have an impact on others that will bring glory to You. In Jesus name, Amen.

Continue writing your prayer here:

Day 2: Intimacy with God Impacts Others

1. What are the 'lions' in your life; things you fear might overtake you?

2. What can you do to build a foundation so when 'lions' come in your life, your faith will be solid?

3. What should your personal application be (at this point in your life), from the story of Daniel in the Lion's Den?

Day 2: JOURNAL

Take a few moments to stop and LISTEN to the Lord; then write down what you sense He is telling you. Is He giving you words of encouragement for yourself that you should note? Is He asking you to encourage or support someone in particular? Is He showing you an adjustment you need to make in your life? Have you seen answered prayers? Write these things down so you create a record of God's goodness to you.

Day 3

Purpose in Communicating with God

Pray: "Lord, show me the secrets you want me to know for Your glory and my good."

Daniel 2 - Excerpts

In the second year of the reign of Nebuchadnezzar, Nebuchadnezzar had dreams; his spirit was troubled, and his sleep left him. ²Then the king commanded that the magicians, the enchanters, the sorcerers, and the Chaldeans be summoned to tell the king his dreams. So they came in and stood before the king. ³And the king said to them, "I had a dream, and my spirit is troubled to know the dream." ⁴Then the Chaldeans said to the king in Aramaic, "O king, live forever! Tell your servants the dream, and we will show the interpretation." ⁵The king answered and said to the Chaldeans, "The word from me is firm: if you do not make known to me the dream and its interpretation, you shall be torn limb from limb, and your houses shall be laid in ruins. ⁶But if you show the dream and its interpretation, you shall receive from me gifts and rewards and great honor. Therefore, show me the dream and its interpretation." ... ¹⁰The Chaldeans answered the king and said, "There is not a man on earth who can meet the king's demand...

¹² Because of this the king was angry and very furious, and commanded that all the wise men of Babylon be destroyed... Then Arioch made the matter known to Daniel. ¹⁶ And Daniel went in and requested the king to appoint him a time, that he might show the interpretation to the king.

¹⁷ Then Daniel went to his house and made the matter known to Hananiah, Mishael, and Azariah, his companions, ¹⁸ and told them to seek mercy from the God of heaven concerning this mystery, so that Daniel and his companions might not be destroyed with the rest of the wise men of Babylon. ¹⁹ Then the mystery was revealed to Daniel in a vision of the night. Then Daniel blessed the God of heaven.

Day 3: Purpose in Communicating with God

Before Daniel ever got thrown to the lions, his life depended on interpreting a dream for King Nebuchadnezzar. The king's edict was: "Interpret the king's dream, without knowing what it was... or die."

Having a real relationship with God, Daniel's first response was to go to God and ask for help.

God loves it when we go to Him with all our concerns, large and small and He loves it even more when we include others. What happened? *Then the secret was revealed to Daniel in a night vision. Daniel 2:19*

What was Daniel's response to God's answer? *So, Daniel blessed the God of heaven. Daniel answered and said: Blessed be the name of God forever and ever, to whom belong wisdom and might.* [21] *He changes times and seasons; he removes kings and sets up kings; he gives wisdom to the wise and knowledge to those who have understanding.* [22] *he reveals deep and hidden things; he knows what is in the darkness, and the light dwells with him.* [23] *To you, O God of my fathers, I give thanks and praise, for you have given me wisdom and might, and have now made known to me what we asked of you, for you have made known to us the king's matter."*

Daniel responded to God by praising Him. What mission has God given you? Who has He asked you to love, minister to, care about? Are you soliciting prayer from friends in the process?

When God gives us purpose and reason for our life, He doesn't just hand it to us and let us go. He is intricately involved in all the details and decisions. When we constantly go to Him and then praise Him for what He accomplishes, He increases our purpose and blesses the work we do.

Prayer:

Dear Lord, thank you for creating me with a purpose. Please give me clarity and wisdom to see what I can do to glorify you. I want to gain understanding of who you are and as a result, who I am. I know you will make known to me what I ask, and I praise you! Amen.

Continue writing your prayer here:

Day 3: Purpose in Communicating with God

1. Has God put a purpose or passion for something in your mind and heart?

2. How can you pray specifically, purposefully, and directly for God's help in what He is asking you to do?

3. Are their people who seem to be conspiring against you? Based on how Daniel responded to them, what should your response be?

Day 3: JOURNAL

Take a few moments to stop and LISTEN to the Lord; then write down what you sense He is telling you. Is He giving you words of encouragement for yourself that you should note? Is He asking you to encourage or support someone in particular? Is He showing you an adjustment you need to make in your life? Have you seen answered prayers? Write these things down so you create a record of God's goodness to you.

Day 4

Understand Communication with God

Pray: "Lord, will you enlighten my understanding where and when I need it to best serve You! Thank You."

Job 42 – (Excerpts)

Then Job answered the Lord and said: I know that you can do everything, and that no purpose of Yours can be withheld from You. You asked, 'Who is this who hides counsel without knowledge?' Therefore I have uttered what I did not understand, things too wonderful for me, which I did not know. Listen, please, and let me speak; You said, 'I will question you, and you shall answer Me.' I have heard of You by the hearing of the ear, But now my eye sees You. Therefore I abhor myself, and repent in dust and ashes. ⁷ After the LORD had spoken these words to Job, the LORD said to Eliphaz the Temanite: "My anger burns against you and against your two friends, for you have not spoken of me what is right, as my servant Job has. ⁸ Now therefore take seven bulls and seven rams and go to my servant Job and offer up a burnt offering for yourselves. And my servant Job shall pray for you, for I will accept his prayer not to deal with you according to your folly. For you have not spoken of me what is right, as my servant Job has." ⁹ So Eliphaz the Temanite and Bildad the Shuhite and Zophar the Naamathite went and did what the LORD had told them, and the LORD accepted Job's prayer.

¹⁰ And the LORD restored the fortunes of Job, when he had prayed for his friends. And the LORD gave Job twice as much as he had before... ¹² And the LORD blessed the latter days of Job more than his beginning... ¹⁵ And in all the land there were no women so beautiful as Job's daughters. And their father gave them an inheritance among their brothers. ¹⁶ And after this Job lived 140 years, and saw his sons, and his sons' sons, four generations. ¹⁷ And Job died, an old man, and full of days.

Day 4: Understand Communication with God

Job 1 tells us what kind of man Job was: *"There was a man in the land of Uz whose name was Job, and that man was blameless and upright, one who feared God and turned away from evil."*

That sounds like the kind of person we want to be. But then horrible things happened to Job. He lost all his children, most of his servants, all his wealth and his health. The truth is none of us want a life with the pain, hurt and loss that Job experienced. But God gives us a front row seat to see not just what happened to Job but more importantly how Job responded to what happened to him.

Job 1:20-22 [20] *Then Job arose and tore his robe and shaved his head and fell on the ground and worshiped.* [21] *And he said, "Naked I came from my mother's womb, and naked shall I return. The L*ORD *gave, and the L*ORD *has taken away; blessed be the name of the L*ORD*."* [22] *In all this Job did not sin or charge God with wrong.*

Job's roadmap gives us freedom to grieve and freedom to feel the pain and express it. But then he moves from the grief to recognition of God, and he turns the grief into worship. This was not joy filled worship. It was the "sacrifice of worship." It's clear that Job's lifestyle was one of worship regardless of the circumstances.

God doesn't immediately change the circumstance, but Job gained understanding and a better perspective of his life. God doesn't answer all the "why" questions; He just shows Job who He is.

Job came to the realization that he can and should trust God even in circumstances beyond his understanding. He was able to say, *"Though He (God) slay me, yet will I trust him."* Determine to turn your lamentations and grief into worship. When you do God will be glorified and you will be blessed. Pray in all times!

Prayer:
God, forgive me for any time I've run from you instead of to you. Forgive me for not understanding you and only focusing on my hurts and problems. Please show me your heart in my circumstances. I acknowledge that your plan is perfect and sovereign. Give me perspective that instead of seeking to avoid trials, I would understand you better in them. In Jesus name, Amen.

Continue writing your prayer here:

Day 4: Understand Communication with God

1. When you are hurt or go through hard things, do you run to or away from God? Why?

2. God is big enough to handle your questions and pain. Do you ask? Do you keep bringing them to Him?

3. What circumstance in your life do you need God's perspective?

When you can't answer "why", search God's character and tell Him you trust Him and His character.

Day 4: JOURNAL

Take a few moments to stop and LISTEN to the Lord; then write down what you sense He is telling you. Is He giving you words of encouragement for yourself that you should note? Is He asking you to encourage or support someone in particular? Is He showing you an adjustment you need to make in your life? Have you seen answered prayers? Write these things down so you create a record of God's goodness to you.

Day 5

The Power in a God Relationship

Pray: "Lord, fill me with Your Spirit, like you did the disciples."

Acts 2 - Excerpts

When the day of Pentecost arrived, they were all together in one place. ² And suddenly there came from heaven a sound like a mighty rushing wind, and it filled the entire house where they were sitting. ³ And divided tongues as of fire appeared to them and rested on each one of them. ⁴ And they were all filled with the Holy Spirit and began to speak in other tongues as the Spirit gave them utterance.

⁵ Now there were dwelling in Jerusalem Jews, devout men from every nation under heaven. ⁶ And at this sound the multitude came together, and they were bewildered, because each one was hearing them speak in his own language. ⁷ And they were amazed and astonished, saying, "Are not all these who are speaking Galileans? ⁸ And how is it that we hear, each of us in his own native language? ⁹ Parthians and Medes and Elamites and residents of Mesopotamia, Judea and Cappadocia, Pontus and Asia, ¹⁰ Phrygia and Pamphylia, Egypt and the parts of Libya belonging to Cyrene, and visitors from Rome, ¹¹ both Jews and proselytes, Cretans and Arabians—we hear them telling in our own tongues the mighty works of God." ¹² And all were amazed and perplexed, saying to one another,

"What does this mean?" ¹³ But others mocking said, "They are filled with new wine."

¹⁴ But Peter, standing with the eleven, lifted up his voice and addressed them: "Men of Judea and all who dwell in Jerusalem, let this be known to you, and give ear to my words. ¹⁵ For these people are not drunk, as you suppose, since it is only the third hour of the day. ¹⁶ But this is what was uttered through the prophet Joel:

¹⁷   "'And in the last days it shall be, God declares, that I will pour out my Spirit on all flesh, and your sons and your daughters shall prophesy, and your young men shall see visions, and your old men shall dream dreams... in those days I will pour out my Spirit, and they shall prophesy.

Day 5: The Power in a God Relationship

We lack the power to create miraculous change in and of ourselves. No matter how much we believe in ourselves, use the power of positive thinking, and try hard, we can't do it. We want to be part of those incredible changes, but it takes more than us. That's why Jesus said in:
Acts 1:8, But you shall receive power when the Holy Spirit has come upon you; and you shall be witnesses to Me in Jerusalem, and in all Judea and Samaria, and to the end of the earth.

Jesus said this because He knew without God's power all he had were 12 ordinary, rather unspectacular and often disbelieving guys. But with the power of God's Holy Spirit, they became the Church. And Jesus made it clear that not even the "gates of hell," will prevail against His Church. If you want to be part of His Church, prayer is non-negotiable, it's a requirement. And being about it consistently and persistently opens the door to the supernatural.
Acts 2:2-4 And suddenly there came a sound from heaven, as of a rushing mighty wind, and it filled the whole house where they were sitting. Then there appeared to them divided tongues, as of fire, and one sat upon each of them. And they were all filled with the Holy Spirit and began to speak with other tongues, as the Spirit gave them utterance.

We demonstrate receptivity through prayer. Knowing God's heart, His will, His Word, makes us able to understand and do miraculous things through Him.

Notice in Acts 2:1 the disciples *"were all with one accord in one place"*. They came together to seek God, believing that He would do great things, and God responded mightily. God answers when we get together in small groups of believers to call on Him in 'one accord'. Who can you get together with to pray?

Prayer:
God, I know you are the same God that showed up on Pentecost; the God who does miraculous things through prayer. Give me discernment and wisdom to know how to pray that I can experience the power of your Holy Spirit. In Jesus name I ask, Amen.

Continue writing your prayer here:

Day 5: The Power in a God Relationship

1. When is a time where your prayers were answered by God working miraculously?

2. What is something you want God to do powerfully in your life or in someone else's?

3. Where have you seen God work this past week? Thank Him here:

Day 5: JOURNAL

Take a few moments to stop and LISTEN to the Lord; then write down what you sense He is telling you. Is He giving you words of encouragement for yourself that you should note? Is He asking you to encourage or support someone in particular? Is He showing you an adjustment you need to make in your life? Have you seen answered prayers? Write these things down so you create a record of God's goodness to you.

Day 6

God and My Ups and Downs

Pray: "Lord, give me Your perspective of my circumstances."

James 1:2-17

Count it all joy, my brothers, when you meet trials of various kinds, ³ for you know that the testing of your faith produces steadfastness. ⁴ And let steadfastness have its full effect, that you may be perfect and complete, lacking in nothing.

⁵ If any of you lacks wisdom, let him ask God, who gives generously to all without reproach, and it will be given him. ⁶ But let him ask in faith, with no doubting, for the one who doubts is like a wave of the sea that is driven and tossed by the wind. ⁷ For that person must not suppose that he will receive anything from the Lord; ⁸ he is a double-minded man, unstable in all his ways.

⁹ Let the lowly brother boast in his exaltation, ¹⁰ and the rich in his humiliation, because like a flower of the grass he will pass away. ¹¹ For the sun rises with its scorching heat and withers the grass; its flower falls, and its beauty perishes. So also will the rich man fade away in the midst of his pursuits.

¹² Blessed is the man who remains steadfast under trial, for when he has stood the test he will receive the crown of life, which God has promised to those who love him. ¹³ Let no one say when he is tempted, "I am being tempted by

God," for God cannot be tempted with evil, and he himself tempts no one. ¹⁴ But each person is tempted when he is lured and enticed by his own desire. ¹⁵ Then desire when it has conceived gives birth to sin, and sin when it is fully grown brings forth death.

¹⁶ Do not be deceived, my beloved brothers. ¹⁷ Every good gift and every perfect gift is from above, coming down from the Father of lights, with whom there is no variation or shadow due to change. Of his own will he brought us forth by the word of truth, that we should be a kind of first fruits of his creatures.

Day 6: God and My Ups and Downs

My brethren, count it all joy when you fall into various trials, knowing that the testing of your faith produces patience. But let patience have its perfect work, that you may be perfect and complete, lacking nothing. James 1:2-6

How can James say such things?! Joy in trials? Glad when our faith is tested? Is James completely unrealistic? Is this attainable or a lofty statement I can't relate to?

James can say this because James *knows* the heart of God. He communes with God in prayer and has had experiences that have drawn him closer to God. You and I can know that as well.

The kind of faith that James is talking about isn't instant. Faith grows and prayer grows as our relationship with God grows. As all relationships, it is strengthened through time and experiences.

When faith is new and a trial comes, we say, "Oh boy, how will this go? I don't know if I can hang on." Then we see how God is faithful and we see patience develop. Later we can say, "This isn't fun, but I know God's got a reason and I suppose I'll be patient by the end!" Later still we say, "Even though this is tough, I am really excited to see what God's going to do."

James *doesn't* mean for us to put on a fake smile, make light of hard situations and say "God is good" through gritted teeth. He *does* mean we must recognize God's ability to use trials to develop good things. God does not leave us hanging but grounds us so that we can manage life's ups and downs with and through His strength.

Prayer:
Lord Jesus, I acknowledge that you can use trials and life's ups and downs to produce patience in me and grow my relationship with you.
Please use _____
(Something in life you are struggling with.)
to produce patience in me. I ask that you give me wisdom and ground me in you so that I don't get tossed about when life happens. Amen.

Continue writing your prayer here:

Day 6: God and My Ups and Downs

1. Do you ever feel pressure to paste on a smile, even when hurting, to look more "spiritual"? Why?

2. What is your typical response to ups and downs in your life?

3. How can you improve your response to life's ups and downs?

Day 6: JOURNAL

Take a few moments to stop and LISTEN to the Lord; then write down what you sense He is telling you. Is He giving you words of encouragement for yourself that you should note? Is He asking you to encourage or support someone in particular? Is He showing you an adjustment you need to make in your life? Have you seen answered prayers? Write these things down so you create a record of God's goodness to you.

Day 7

The Pathway to Help from God

Pray: "Lord, show me how you are my help and deliverer."

Scripture: Psalm 30

I will extol you, O LORD, for you have drawn me up
>and have not let my foes rejoice over me.
2 O LORD my God, I cried to you for help,
>and you have healed me.
3 O LORD, you have brought up my soul from Sheol;
>you restored me to life from among those who go
>>down to the pit.
4 Sing praises to the LORD, O you his saints,
>and give thanks to his holy name.
5 For his anger is but for a moment,
>and his favor is for a lifetime.
>Weeping may tarry for the night,
>but joy comes with the morning.
6 As for me, I said in my prosperity,
>"I shall never be moved."
7 By your favor, O LORD,
>you made my mountain stand strong;
>you hid your face;
>>I was dismayed.
8 To you, O LORD, I cry,
>and to the Lord I plead for mercy:
9 "What profit is there in my death,

>   if I go down to the pit?
>   Will the dust praise you?
>   Will it tell of your faithfulness?
> 10 Hear, O LORD, and be merciful to me!
>   O LORD, be my helper!"
> 11 You have turned for me my mourning into dancing;
>   you have loosed my sackcloth
>   and clothed me with gladness,
> 12 that my glory may sing your praise and not be silent.
>   O LORD my God, I will give thanks to you forever!

Day 7: The Pathway to Help from God

I love it when God answers my prayers the way I want Him to and when He does it quickly. It's easy to get used to that and to expect it. But the Psalmist makes it clear that sometimes we must wait patiently on the Lord. But the picture here is not one of doing nothing while we wait. We need to keep praying and keep praying and then ask Him to show us what else to keep praying about.

When we trust God and keep praying, He will often do what He did for the Psalmist in Psalm 30. He'll give us a new song to sing, and we will find ourselves singing a song of praise to our God. Did you know that your singing can also be a prayer? I love the fact that God isn't put off by our talent in singing. He loves it when we sing to him regardless of the quality of our voice or our ability to stay on key.

Sometimes we run short of things to say to God. If you find yourself short on words, consider praying the scripture. Praying the scripture allows us to put into our own words what other believers have prayed in the past. Today's scripture reading from Psalm 30 is a great one to pray out loud and personally to God. Try doing that and when you do it make sure you are sincere in your prayer. When we pray with sincerity and passion, we will often find ourselves ending our prayers just like the Psalmist so often do by saying, "GREAT IS THE LORD!"

Prayer:

Lord Jesus, thank You that I have the privilege of praying to You and that You hear me. Help me to be patient and to continue to pray for those things that You put on my heart because the Holy Spirit is inside of me. Show me if there are things you want to change in me and give me the courage and strength to make those changes. And Lord, I'm praying for those assignments you might have for me in the next days and week. Give me eyes to see them, courage to carry out what You have for me to do and give me the joy that comes from partnering with You in Your Kingdom work. Lord Jesus, show me those you want me to encourage this week and show me how to do that in a way that will be for their good and Your glory. Thanks for all You have done for me. In Jesus name, Amen.

Continue writing your prayer here:

Day 7: The Pathway to Help from God

1. What things have you learned from God this past week?

2. How has this past week affected your prayer life?

3. Is there something you have learned or prayed about that you can practically apply to your life?

Day 7: JOURNAL

Take a few moments to stop and LISTEN to the Lord; then write down what you sense He is telling you. Is He giving you words of encouragement and support for yourself that you should note? Is He asking you to encourage or support someone in particular? Is He showing you an adjustment you need to make in your life? Have you seen answered prayers? Write these things down so you create a record of God's goodness to you.

Day 8

Setting the Stage

Pray: "Lord, let me adore you in words and actions today. Show me how to adore Your name."

Scripture: Matthew 6:5-15

"And when you pray, you must not be like the hypocrites. For they love to stand and pray in the synagogues and at the street corners, that they may be seen by others. Truly, I say to you, they have received their reward. ⁶ But when you pray, go into your room and shut the door and pray to your Father who is in secret. And your Father who sees in secret will reward you.

⁷ "And when you pray, do not heap up empty phrases as the Gentiles do, for they think that they will be heard for their many words. ⁸ Do not be like them, for your Father knows what you need before you ask him. ⁹ Pray then like this:

"Our Father in heaven,
hallowed be your name.
10 Your kingdom come,
your will be done,
 on earth as it is in heaven.
11 Give us this day our daily bread,
12 and forgive us our debts,

>   as we also have forgiven our debtors.
> 13 And lead us not into temptation,
>   but deliver us from evil.

¹⁴ For if you forgive others their trespasses, your heavenly Father will also forgive you, ¹⁵ but if you do not forgive others their trespasses, neither will your Father forgive your trespasses.

Day 8: Setting the Stage

The Lord reigns, he is clothed with majesty; the Lord is clothed, He has girded Himself with strength. Surely the world is established, so that it cannot be moved. Your throne is established from of old; You are from everlasting. Psalm 93:1,2

The Psalmist knows who God is and where his focus should be. The beginning of the Lord's Prayer, our model prayer, also states who God is because it brings glory to the One who deserves it, and it reminds us of our place. We remind ourselves of why He is worthy.

Adoring God when we pray keeps us in check. It prevents us from constantly coming to him with our requests list. Our focus gets switched from "me me me" to "I'm talking to my Holy God and in relationship with Him." He is so worthy to be praised and adored even if He never gives me anything.

"Praise the Lord! Oh give thanks to the Lord, for He is good! For His mercy endures forever." Psalm 106:1

David was a man's man; the kind of man that kills a giant with a stone, defeats whole armies, and rules a nation. Even he knew that he was nothing without God and that God was the reason for his success. In fact, he begs God never to leave him or forsake him. This realization is reflected in his constant adoration weaving through the Psalms.

Prayer:
Fill in the following with words of adoration:
Lord, my Father, you are _____! I adore you because _____. I believe you are worthy of my adoration because _____
_____
Thank you for _____.

Confess to Him if your prayers have been 'me' centered.

Continue writing your prayer here:

Day 8: Setting the Stage

1. Do you take time to adore the Lord when you pray? If so, how?

2. Do you believe He is worthy to be adored? Why or why not?

3. Do your prayers demonstrate that you expect God to serve you, or do you serve him?

4. In what way do your prayers reflect who you serve?

Day 8: JOURNAL

Take a few moments to stop and LISTEN to the Lord; then write down what you sense He is telling you. Is He giving you words of encouragement and support for yourself that you should note? Is He asking you to encourage or support someone in particular? Is He showing you an adjustment you need to make in your life? Have you seen answered prayers? Write these things down so you create a record of God's goodness to you.

Day 9

Affirming the Positions

Pray: *"Lord, show me why it's good to have You as MY Lord."*

Scripture: Psalm 18 – (Excerpts)

The LORD is my rock and my fortress and my deliverer,
  my God, my rock, in whom I take refuge,
  my shield, and the horn of my salvation, my
    stronghold.
³ I call upon the LORD, who is worthy to be praised,
  and I am saved from my enemies.
⁶ In my distress I called upon the LORD;
  to my God I cried for help.
From his temple he heard my voice,
  and my cry to him reached his ears.
¹⁶ He sent from on high, he took me;
  he drew me out of many waters.
¹⁷ He rescued me from my strong enemy
  and from those who hated me,
  for they were too mighty for me.
¹⁹ He brought me out into a broad place;
  he rescued me, because he delighted in me.
⁴⁶ The LORD lives, and blessed be my rock,
  and exalted be the God of my salvation—

Affirming the Positions

"The law of the Lord is perfect, converting the soul; the testimony of the Lord is sure, making wise the simple; The fear of the Lord is clean, enduring forever; the judgments of the Lord are true and righteous altogether." Psalm 19:7,9

By saying "Thy kingdom come thy will be done" we are affirming the Lordship of God. We recognize His place and as a result also come to know our place in light of His Lordship. This God can be really scary for those that want to hurt his children. But He is incredibly loving and gentle with those who love Him.

David had a grasp on celebrating who God is. He rejoiced in the fact that God knows best and is in charge. David recognized that God was his covering and Lord even though he himself was a powerful king. Instead of being threatened by God's might, he is empowered by it.

It's easy to buy into the line of thinking that says, "I'm the boss of me. Nobody tells me what to do." Affirming God's Lordship in our life is saying, "You are the boss of me. You tell me what to do and I'm thankful."

God is not only Lord, but He is a good God involved in our life. Psalm 27:1 says, *"The Lord is my light and my salvation; whom shall I fear? The Lord is the strength of my life; of whom shall I be afraid?"* Take comfort that God is your boss. He only fills that role when you let Him but when He does the only thing you need to do is be obedient and he will lead you with a strength that you can't muster up in yourself. You will never be more free, more fulfilled, and more empowered than when you are following Him and being obedient to Him. Let Him lead, direct and fight for you.

Prayer:
Lord, I know you are Lord of everything in heaven and earth. You are Lord of my life. I am thankful that it's your kingdom and your will be done. Please show me today how to allow your Lordship in my daily life. In Jesus name, Amen.

Continue writing your prayer here:

Day 9: Affirming the Positions

"Thy kingdom come thy will be done on earth as it is in heaven."

1. What makes you confident that the Lord can be Lord of your life?

2. How do you allow Him control over your life and circumstances?

3. Affirming God's Lordship is more than words, prayers, or saying we believe. What action is He calling you to, to demonstrate that He is Lord in your life?

Day 9: JOURNAL

Take a few moments to stop and LISTEN to the Lord; then write down what you sense He is telling you. Is He giving you words of encouragement and support for yourself that you should note? Is He asking you to encourage or support someone in particular? Is He showing you an adjustment you need to make in your life? Have you seen answered prayers? Write these things down so you create a record of God's goodness to you.

Day 10

Presenting Requests

Pray: "Lord, give me peace with knowing that I need to come to you daily in order to be healthy and fed."

Scripture: Psalm 5

Give ear to my words, O Lord; consider my groaning.
2 Give attention to the sound of my cry,
 my King and my God, for to you do I pray.
3 O Lord, in the morning you hear my voice;
 in the morning I prepare a sacrifice for you and watch.
4 For you are not a God who delights in wickedness;
 evil may not dwell with you.
5 The boastful shall not stand before your eyes;
 you hate all evildoers.
6 You destroy those who speak lies;
 the Lord abhors the bloodthirsty and deceitful man.
7 But I, through the abundance of your steadfast love, will enter your house.
 I will bow down toward your holy temple in the fear of you.
8 Lead me, O Lord, in your righteousness because of my enemies; make your way straight before me.

9 For there is no truth in their mouth; their inmost self
    is destruction; their throat is an open grave;
    they flatter with their tongue.
10 Make them bear their guilt, O God; let them fall by
    their own counsels; because of the abundance
    of their transgressions cast them out, for they
    have rebelled against you.
11 But let all who take refuge in you rejoice;
    let them ever sing for joy,
  and spread your protection over them,
    that those who love your name may exult in you.
12 For you bless the righteous, O LORD;
    you cover him with favor as with a shield.

Day 10: Presenting Requests
"Give us this day our daily bread."

Give ear to my words, O Lord, consider my meditation. Give heed to the voice of my cry, My King and my God, for to you I will pray. My voice You shall hear in the morning, O Lord; In the morning I will direct it to you, and I will look up. Psalm 5:1-3

God already knows our needs, but He wants us to communicate them to Him. His desire is to have a relationship with us. When we make requests, we get to see God answer. And God is interested in us doing this as a daily thing. The picture here is one of the manna in the wilderness for the Israelites. They had to collect it each and every day. God wants us to have daily interaction with Him.

The Lord's intentions for us are bigger than just a string of answered requests. He builds our faith, He allows us to experience His hand, to understand His will, and gives us opportunity to rejoice in who He is- not just merely what we can get from Him.

When you come to present requests to God, how do you approach Him? Do you half-heartedly go through the motions of routine prayer, without anticipating or expecting much? Do you see Him as your Genie, or do you recognize Him as the God of the Universe who actually hears your prayers and responds to them?

David asked with his whole heart. *"Lord, I cry out to you; make haste to me! Give ear to my voice when I cry out to You. Let my prayer be set before You as incense, the lifting up of my hands as the evening sacrifice." Psalm 141:1,2*

Do you present requests only hoping for a quick answer? Or do you ask with the intention to know God more because of your prayers? Ask God to reveal Himself more and more to you.

Prayer:
Lord, I want what you want for me. I want to make my requests to you and not only have answers but know you more and grow in my faith as a result. As I make my requests known, please show me the big picture.

Continue writing your prayer here:

Day 10: Presenting Requests

1. Have you ever prayed fervently; desperately for something? Not just rattling off a list but truly, diligently seeking. When?

2. What happened?

3. When is a time God has answered your prayer/s?

4. How close was it to what you expected?

Day 10: JOURNAL

Take a few moments to stop and LISTEN to the Lord; then write down what you sense He is telling you. Is He giving you words of encouragement and support for yourself that you should note? Is He asking you to encourage or support someone in particular? Is He showing you an adjustment you need to make in your life? Have you seen answered prayers? Write these things down so you create a record of God's goodness to you.

Also: Spend time making your requests known to the Lord. Share your deepest questions and wait to understand.

Day 11

Clearing the Static

Pray: "Lord will you forgive me and help me to forgive others."

Scripture: Psalm 32

Blessed is the one whose transgression is forgiven,
   whose sin is covered.
2 Blessed is the man against whom the LORD counts no iniquity,
   and in whose spirit there is no deceit.
3 For when I kept silent, my bones wasted away
   through my groaning all day long.
4 For day and night your hand was heavy upon me;
   my strength was dried up as by the heat of summer. *Selah*
5 I acknowledged my sin to you,
   and I did not cover my iniquity;
I said, "I will confess my transgressions to the LORD,"
   and you forgave the iniquity of my sin. *Selah*
6 Therefore let everyone who is godly
   offer prayer to you at a time when you may be found;
surely in the rush of great waters,
   they shall not reach him.
7 You are a hiding place for me;
   you preserve me from trouble;

you surround me with shouts of deliverance. *Selah*
8 I will instruct you and teach you in the way you should go;
I will counsel you with my eye upon you.
9 Be not like a horse or a mule, without understanding,
which must be curbed with bit and bridle,
or it will not stay near you.
10 Many are the sorrows of the wicked,
but steadfast love surrounds the one who trusts in the Lord.
11 Be glad in the Lord, and rejoice, O righteous,
and shout for joy, all you upright in heart!

Day 11: Clearing the Static

"Forgive us our debts as we forgive our debtors..."

If you, Lord, should mark iniquities, O Lord, who could stand? But there is forgiveness with You, that You may be feared. Psalm 130:3,4

Often in our culture we overlook the severity of sin. We say, "I'm good enough" or "I'm better than that guy over there" or "I try hard. That's worth something, isn't it?" or "A for effort!"

To understand the severity of sin, read Psalm 32:3-5. David is descriptive in what sin does when it eats away at us. He talks about how his "bones grew old" and God's "hand heavy upon me."

No one is exempt. Sin is anything that separates us from having a relationship with God. It is anything wrong that we do or even think. It is our pain, our blindness, and leads to our death.

But there is hope! We have a trustworthy God! Many religions only hope that their god will be good. They worship cold idols or dead men and try in vain to please impersonal gods or to earn forgiveness by works.

Our God is the True, Living God. He isn't cold or impersonal. We know His heart and that He is trustworthy by what He has done, sending His Son to die for us. When we confess our sins, He promises to forgive us. We don't have to second guess or fear our fate. God clearly lays it out for us in His Word.

If you have accepted Jesus Christ as your Savior, God doesn't even see your sin! What He sees instead is the righteousness of Jesus, which has been credited to you. It's no wonder Jesus is called our "Redeemer." He's paid the price for us to be redeemed!

Prayer:

Dear God, I recognize that sin is serious. I'm sorry if I've ever taken it lightly. Lord, I also recognize that you made a serious sacrifice of your Son so that I don't have to live with the 'groaning' that sin brings. Thank you, Lord, that I can stand because there is forgiveness in Jesus Christ. In Jesus name, Amen.

Ask God to show you anything in your life that you need to confess to Him.

Continue writing your prayer here:

Day 11: Clearing the Static

"Forgive us our debts as we forgive our debtors…"

1. Do you take sin and forgiveness lightly? How should you view it?

2. Do you confess your sins? How?

3. Read Psalm 32:3-5. Have you ever experienced what David describes? If so, what was it like?

Day 11: JOURNAL

Take a few moments to stop and LISTEN to the Lord; then write down what you sense He is telling you. Is He giving you words of encouragement and support for yourself that you should note? Is He asking you to encourage or support someone in particular? Is He showing you an adjustment you need to make in your life? Have you seen answered prayers? Write these things down so you create a record of God's goodness to you.

Also: Spend time making your requests known to the Lord. Share your deepest questions and wait to understand.

Day 12

Establishing Direction

Pray: "Lord, forgive me and help me to forgive."

Scripture: Psalm 51:1-12

Have mercy on me, O God,
    according to your steadfast love;
according to your abundant mercy
    blot out my transgressions.
2 Wash me thoroughly from my iniquity,
    and cleanse me from my sin!
3 For I know my transgressions,
    and my sin is ever before me.
4 Against you, you only, have I sinned
    and done what is evil in your sight,
so that you may be justified in your words
    and blameless in your judgment.
5 Behold, I was brought forth in iniquity,
    and in sin did my mother conceive me.
6 Behold, you delight in truth in the inward being,
    and you teach me wisdom in the secret heart.
7 Purge me with hyssop, and I shall be clean;
    wash me, and I shall be whiter than snow.
8 Let me hear joy and gladness;
    let the bones that you have broken rejoice.
9 Hide your face from my sins,
    and blot out all my iniquities.

10 Create in me a clean heart, O God,
    and renew a right spirit within me.
11 Cast me not away from your presence,
    and take not your Holy Spirit from me.
12 Restore to me the joy of your salvation,
    and uphold me with a willing spirit

13 Then I will teach transgressors your ways,
    and sinners will return to you.
14 Deliver me from blood guiltiness, O God,
   O God of my salvation,
    and my tongue will sing aloud of your righteousness.
15 O Lord, open my lips,
    and my mouth will declare your praise.

Day 12: Establishing Direction

"Lead me not into temptation but deliver me from evil..."

For I acknowledge my transgressions, and my sin is always before me. Against You, You only, have I sinned, and done this evil in Your sight- that You may be found just when You speak, and blameless when you judge. Psalm 51:3-4

This is David's prayer after he has committed adultery and murder. God sent a prophet, Nathan, to bring David's sin to his attention. David was convicted, broken, and probably embarrassed and disgusted with himself. He needed forgiveness himself and he needed to forgive others.

But praise God! The weight of his sin and being confronted with it in a very public way, brought David to the point of confessing, which is what he is doing in these verses. He chose to ask God to cover his sin with forgiveness instead of letting himself give in to guilt and shame. He asks, *"Purge me with hyssop, and I shall be clean; wash me and I shall be whiter than snow."*

David's process of confession was to recognize sin and confess it (verses 3,4), request God's cleansing (verses 7,8), praise God (verse 15) and then acknowledge that God can use even the ugliest sin to further His kingdom (verses 12,13).

But in the Lord's prayer Jesus gives a caveat to our sin being forgiven… even after asking. He says we need to forgive others as well. He said that if we do not forgive others their sins then our Father in Heaven will not forgive our sins. That should be motivation enough to forgive others. Psychologists also tell us that forgiving others benefits the one forgiving more than the one forgiven. Plenty of good reasons to do the hard thing.

Prayer:
Ask God to convict you of any wrong action, motive, or attitude. Confess your sin. Ask God to give you a clean heart.
Thank Him! Ask Him to give you the opportunity to use this to bring Him glory and help someone else.

Continue writing your prayer here:

Day 12: Establishing Direction

"Lead me not into temptation but deliver me from evil..."

1. Do you have an already forgiven sin you cover with guilt instead of living in God's grace? If so, name it and ask God to take away the guilt since He has forgiven the sin.

2. What have you learned from this Psalm that you can apply to your prayer life?

3. Ask the Holy Spirit to bring to mind anyone that you need to forgive and then ask for the ability and determination to do it. What can make this difficult?

If you've been forgiven, don't let guilt and shame creep back into your mind. Memorize Romans 6:14, *"For sin shall not have dominion over you, for you are not under law but under grace."*

Day 12: JOURNAL

Take a few moments to stop and LISTEN to the Lord; then write down what you sense He is telling you. Is He giving you words of encouragement and support for yourself that you should note? Is He asking you to encourage or support someone in particular? Is He showing you an adjustment you need to make in your life? Have you seen answered prayers? Write these things down so you create a record of God's goodness to you.

Day 13

Connecting the Power

Pray: "Lord, show me reasons to praise You joyfully."

Scripture: Matthew 26:6-16

Now when Jesus was at Bethany in the house of Simon the leper, [7] a woman came up to him with an alabaster flask of very expensive ointment, and she poured it on his head as he reclined at table. [8] And when the disciples saw it, they were indignant, saying, "Why this waste? [9] For this could have been sold for a large sum and given to the poor." [10] But Jesus, aware of this, said to them, "Why do you trouble the woman? For she has done a beautiful thing to me. [11] For you always have the poor with you, but you will not always have me. [12] In pouring this ointment on my body, she has done it to prepare me for burial. [13] Truly, I say to you, wherever this gospel is proclaimed in the whole world, what she has done will also be told in memory of her."

Read Psalm 106:1-5

Day 13: Connecting the Power

"For thine is the kingdom, and the power, and the glory forever."

For the Lord is the great God, and the great King above all gods. In His hand are the deep places of the earth; the heights of the hills are His also. The sea is His, for He made it; and His hands formed the dry land. Psalm 95:3-5

David knew how to unashamedly praise God. In 2 Samuel 6:16 his wife Michal is embarrassed at the way he leaps and dances in front of the Lord. God loves praise and takes it seriously. He demonstrates this when He punishes Michal for despising David's worship. David response is to say, "I will celebrate before the Lord!" What he was doing was dancing for God… just a thought.

In Matthew 26:7-13 a woman pours oil on Jesus' head. He receives and values her praise. In fact, He rebukes the disciples when they think the woman wasted costly oil. Jesus knows that the most significant thing she can do is express praise the way it's on her heart to express it. *"Why do you trouble the woman? For she has done a good work for me." Matthew 26:10*

Praise doesn't have to be limited to a quick blessing at mealtime or church worship, much like romance isn't limited to red roses and candlelight. God has given you gifts and interests to be used to praise Him. Maybe you express your praise through singing in the car, hiking, writing poetry, or taking the back roads on a motorcycle. Whatever God has given you as a resource or ability, use it to express praise. Get creative and enjoy your time with the Lord!

Prayer:
Lord, I want to praise you regardless of what others think. I want to honor You and recognize Your greatness. You ARE good and your mercy and kindness to me are amazing and worth dancing about! Be honored by my praise of you and show me how I can honor you throughout this day. Be glorified, In Jesus name, Amen.

Continue writing your prayer here:

Day 13: Connecting the Power

1. What interests and passions has God given you?

2. How can you use those things to praise Him?

3. How are you willing to look foolish like David and the woman with the oil, to please God?

Day 13: JOURNAL

Take a few moments to stop and LISTEN to the Lord; then write down what you sense He is telling you. Is He giving you words of encouragement and support for yourself that you should note? Is He asking you to encourage or support someone in particular? Is He showing you an adjustment you need to make in your life? Have you seen answered prayers? Write these things down so you create a record of God's goodness to you.

Day 14

Reflecting on the Manual

Pray: "Lord help me to live my life fully for you."

Psalm 119 - Excerpts

Blessed are those whose way is blameless, who walk in the law of the Lord! ² Blessed are those who keep his testimonies, who seek him with their whole heart, ³ who also do no wrong, but walk in his ways! ⁴ You have commanded your precepts to be kept diligently.
⁵ Oh that my ways may be steadfast in keeping your statutes! Then I shall not be put to shame, having my eyes fixed on all your commandments. ⁷ I will praise you with an upright heart, when I learn your righteous rules. ⁸ I will keep your statutes; do not utterly forsake me! ¹⁰ With my whole heart I seek you; let me not wander from your commandments!

¹¹ I have stored up your word in my heart, that I might not sin against you. ¹² Blessed are you, O Lord; teach me your statutes! ¹³ With my lips I declare all the rules of your mouth. ¹⁴ In the way of your testimonies I delight as much as in all riches. ¹⁵ I will meditate on your precepts and fix my eyes on your ways. ¹⁶ I will delight in your statutes; I will not forget your word. ¹⁷ Deal bountifully with your servant, that I may live and keep your word. ¹⁸ Open my eyes, that I may behold wondrous things out of your law. ¹⁹ I am a sojourner on the earth; hide not your

commandments from me! [20] My soul is consumed with longing for your rules at all times. [21] You rebuke the insolent, accursed ones, who wander from your commandments. [22] Take away from me scorn and contempt, for I have kept your testimonies. [33] Teach me, O LORD, the way of your statutes; and I will keep it to the end. [34] Give me understanding, that I may keep your law and observe it with my whole heart. [35] Lead me in the path of your commandments, for I delight in it. [36] Incline my heart to your testimonies, and not to selfish gain! [37] Turn my eyes from looking at worthless things; and give me life in your ways.

Day 14: Reflecting on the Manual

Psalm 119 is the longest Psalm in the Bible, by quite a bit. And it's all about loving God's words, His teachings, His commands, His statutes, His law, and His testimonies. Read the psalm in its entirety and you'll hear the theme ringing through it over and over again. There are some things here that are very important for us to understand about God.

Prayer, studying God's word (the Bible) and listening to God's Word (through the Holy Spirit) are the best ways to get to know God more. And the more we know God the more in love with God we will become.

It's so important to understand that God IS love; He personifies it, He defines it and He demonstrates it. When we really understand that as His character and what defines Him, we will see His decisions and actions from the perspective of love.

God gave His commandments, His teachings, His statutes out of love. He loves us so much that He wants us to enjoy our lives to the fullest and see Him in each part of our lives. We will not do that and cannot do that if we don't understand His character of love and grace.

I wish I was the perfect dad. Not so much because I aspire to be perfect personally but because I want to afford my children the absolute best opportunities for them to be all God has created them to be. Simply put, I want the best for them.

Our God is a perfect God. And that God actually, truly, and perfectly wants the best for you. He wants you to do each and every part of your life in partnership with Him. That cannot be done if you don't intentionally and purposefully stay connected to Him. We really do need to put our aspirations into action.

Prayer:
My Father in Heaven, I want to live my life more fully for You and with You. Would you let me see you in even the little things of life and would you increase my appreciation for Your love for me. I thank You and bless You for being such a loving father. In Jesus name, Amen.

Continue writing your prayer here:

Day 14: Reflecting on the Manual
Look over the last 6 days of devotions

1. What new things have you learned this past week?

2. How has this week affected your prayer life?

3. What have you learned or prayed about that you can practically apply to your life?

:

Day 14: JOURNAL

Take a few moments to stop and LISTEN to the Lord; then write down what you sense He is telling you. Is He giving you words of encouragement and support for yourself that you should note? Is He asking you to encourage or support someone in particular? Is He showing you an adjustment you need to make in your life? Have you seen answered prayers? Write these things down so you create a record of God's goodness to you.

Day 15

Telling the Truth

Pray: "Lord, show me what THE truth is by Your word."

Scripture: John 8:31-47

So Jesus said to the Jews who had believed him, "If you abide in my word, you are truly my disciples, ³² and you will know the truth, and the truth will set you free." ³³ They answered him, "We are offspring of Abraham and have never been enslaved to anyone. How is it that you say, 'You will become free'?"

³⁴ Jesus answered them, "Truly, truly, I say to you, everyone who practices sin is a slave to sin. ³⁵ The slave does not remain in the house forever; the son remains forever. ³⁶ So if the Son sets you free, you will be free indeed. ³⁷ I know that you are offspring of Abraham; yet you seek to kill me because my word finds no place in you. ³⁸ I speak of what I have seen with my Father, and you do what you have heard from your father."

³⁹ They answered him, "Abraham is our father." Jesus said to them, "If you were Abraham's children, you would be doing the works Abraham did, ⁴⁰ but now you seek to kill me, a man who has told you the truth that I heard from God. This is not what Abraham did. ⁴¹ You are doing the works your father did." They said to him, "We were not born of sexual immorality. We have one Father—even God." ⁴² Jesus said to them, "If God were your Father, you

would love me, for I came from God and I am here. I came not of my own accord, but he sent me. ⁴³ Why do you not understand what I say? It is because you cannot bear to hear my word. ⁴⁴ You are of your father the devil, and your will is to do your father's desires. He was a murderer from the beginning, and does not stand in the truth, because there is no truth in him. When he lies, he speaks out of his own character, for he is a liar and the father of lies. ⁴⁵ But because I tell the truth, you do not believe me. ⁴⁶ Which one of you convicts me of sin? If I tell the truth, why do you not believe me? ⁴⁷ Whoever is of God hears the words of God. The reason why you do not hear them is that you are not of God."

Day 15: Telling the Truth

"Stand having fastened on the belt of truth..."

Jesus said to him, "I am the way, the truth, and the life. No one comes to the Father except through Me." John 14:6

Many people say that truth is objective. Others claim truth is what can be proven scientifically. Some believe that we can't know anything for sure unless it can be seen empirically. There are people who wouldn't even go that far, saying everything is subjective; "What is true for me might not be true for you. Everyone can choose their own truth."

Truth does not change if you don't believe it. If I believe the world is flat you would tell me that what I believe doesn't matter. The world is round and that's a fact regardless of my opinion.

In a muddled world and a muddled time, how can we really know Truth? CNN tells me something different than ABC and they both don't agree with New York Times. What am I to believe?

"Then Jesus said to those Jews who believed Him, "If you abide in My word, you are my disciples indeed. And you shall know the truth and the truth shall make you free." John 8:31

We fasten on the belt of truth by knowing the Word of God, which is truth. Abiding in the Bible and knowing Jesus will bring clarity and freedom because the truth of Jesus Christ makes us free. When you question something as true or false, bring your question to the Bible. Does it line up with what God says or does it contradict it?

A caution: When we are dispensing truth, we should always coat it with love and grace. That's why John wrote about Jesus that he was full of grace and truth. The two go together!

Prayer:

Dear Lord, I want the belt of truth around my waist, and I want it to be Your truth not what I might perceive to be true. I don't want to know truth just for knowledge's sake, but so I can apply it to my life. Help me practically put your truth into action in my life today. In Jesus name, Amen.

Continue writing your prayer here:

Day 15: Telling the Truth

"Stand having fastened on the belt of truth…"

1. Why is it important to fasten on the belt of truth?

2. Do you ever feel the truth is hazy? When and why do you feel that way?

3. What are you going to do this week to "fasten on the belt of truth"?

Day 15: JOURNAL

Take a few moments to stop and LISTEN to the Lord; then write down what you sense He is telling you. Is He giving you words of encouragement and support for yourself that you should note? Is He asking you to encourage or support someone in particular? Is He showing you an adjustment you need to make in your life? Have you seen answered prayers? Write these things down so you create a record of God's goodness to you.

Day 16

Protecting the Heart

Pray: "Lord, I value your righteousness. Help me to live with humility in light of your sacrifice."

Scripture: Ephesians 6:11-20

Put on the whole armor of God, that you may be able to stand against the schemes of the devil. [12] For we do not wrestle against flesh and blood, but against the rulers, against the authorities, against the cosmic powers over this present darkness, against the spiritual forces of evil in the heavenly places. [13] Therefore take up the whole armor of God, that you may be able to withstand in the evil day, and having done all, to stand firm. [14] Stand therefore, having fastened on the belt of truth, and having put on the breastplate of righteousness, [15] and, as shoes for your feet, having put on the readiness given by the gospel of peace. [16] In all circumstances take up the shield of faith, with which you can extinguish all the flaming darts of the evil one; [17] and take the helmet of salvation, and the sword of the Spirit, which is the word of God, [18] praying at all times in the Spirit, with prayer and supplication. To that end, keep alert with all perseverance, making supplication for all the saints, [19] and also for me, that words may be given to me in opening my mouth boldly to proclaim the mystery of the gospel, [20] for which I am an ambassador in chains, that I may declare it boldly, as I ought to speak.

Day 16: Protecting the Heart

"The breastplate of righteousness,"

"...and be found in Him, not having my own righteousness, which is from the law, but that which is through faith in Christ, the righteousness which is from God by faith;" Philippians 3:9

Part of the armor of God that we put on is the 'breastplate of righteousness'. Paul explains in Philippians 3:9 that righteousness is not produced from a list of dos and don'ts. It's not something that can be found by performing religious ceremony. We are righteous and get to claim righteousness not because of what we have done but only because of what Jesus has done for us.

In the Old Testament God required sacrifice, something to take sin on itself so His people could be forgiven and righteous. Then He sent His Son, Jesus, to be the final and complete sacrifice. Jesus Christ died taking all our sins on Himself so that we could have righteousness that we could never produce on our own.

When we have faith in Jesus and have been forgiven, that is the lens that God sees us through. Instead of seeing all our sins when He looks at us, God sees us as His Son; perfect and righteous.

"And if Christ is in you, the body is dead because of sin, but the Spirit is life because of righteousness. But if the Spirit of Him who raised Jesus from the dead dwells in you, He who raised Christ from the dead will also give life to your mortal bodies through His Spirit who dwells in you." Romans 8:10,11

Prayer:
Dear Jesus, give me eyes to see how to live in our righteousness this week. I don't want to take for granted what you have done. I want to live in the freedom that your righteousness brings. I am SO thankful that you see me without sin. It's hard to accept that because of what I've done but I do accept it with delight and humility because of what You have done for me. Thank You, thank You, thank You! In Jesus name, Amen.

Continue writing your prayer here:

Day 16: Protecting the Heart

1. Have you tried to 'earn' righteousness? How?

2. How do you gain true righteousness?

3. What does the 'breastplate of righteousness' look like in your life this week?

Day 16: JOURNAL

Take a few moments to stop and LISTEN to the Lord; then write down what you sense He is telling you. Is He giving you words of encouragement and support for yourself that you should note? Is He asking you to encourage or support someone in particular? Is He showing you an adjustment you need to make in your life? Have you seen answered prayers? Write these things down so you create a record of God's goodness to you.

Day 17

Praying in Peace

Pray: "Lord, let me experience and understand Your peace."

Scripture: Ezekiel 37:26-28

I will make a covenant of peace with them. It shall be an everlasting covenant with them. And I will set them in their land and multiply them and will set my sanctuary in their midst forevermore. ²⁷ My dwelling place shall be with them, and I will be their God, and they shall be my people. ²⁸ Then the nations will know that I am the Lord who sanctifies Israel, when my sanctuary is in their midst forevermore."

Scripture: Isaiah 9:6-7

⁶ For to us a child is born, to us a son is given;
    and the government shall be upon his shoulder,
      and his name shall be called
    Wonderful Counselor, Mighty God,
      Everlasting Father, Prince of Peace.
⁷   Of the increase of his government and of peace
      there will be no end,
   on the throne of David and over his kingdom,
      to establish it and to uphold it
   with justice and with righteousness
      from this time forth and forevermore.
   The zeal of the Lord of hosts will do this.

Day 17: Praying in Peace

"...and having shod your feet with the preparation of the gospel of peace." Ephesians 6:15

Peace. What an interesting thing to add to battle plan.. Wearing peace on our feet helps us in battle? This verse in Ephesians explains that Jesus is our peace because He has broken down the wall between us and God. He has created peace between us and God because He has offered us forgiveness and a way to be pure so that our broken relationship with God can be restored.

For He Himself is our peace, who has made both one, and has broken down the middle wall of separation. Ephesians 2:14

When we are involved in a battle, how can we have peace in our souls? Battle brings thoughts of death, of confrontation, of hard decisions, and the fear of losing.

"These things I have spoken to you, that in Me you may have peace. In the world you will have tribulation; but be of good cheer, I have overcome the world." John 16:33

We are on the winning side! We can have peace because we have the assurance that even though we might at times feel like we are losing, even though we will face hard things while we are on earth, ultimately Jesus Christ has overcome the world. Be confident when you pray and slip peace on your feet.

Prayer:

Dear Lord, I don't want to be rocked, swayed, or uptight. I want the peace of God that transcends all understanding. Will you give me the ability to have peace in _____.

(Situation or relationship where peace is needed)

I praise you for being a God that brings assurance and peace to my life. And Lord, while I'm thinking of peace, I can't help but think of _____, who doesn't seem to have any peace. Please let me be a person of peace to them and would you make yourself so real to them that they feel the peace of your presence in their lives. Thank you, Jesus! In Your name I pray, Amen.

Continue writing your prayer here:

Day 17: Praying in Peace

1. When is a time you have experienced the peace of God?

2. What area of your life do you need peace in right now?

3. Who do you know that really needs peace right now? Pray for them specifically and write it here so when God answers you can record that as well.

Day 17: JOURNAL

Take a few moments to stop and LISTEN to the Lord; then write down what you sense He is telling you. Is He giving you words of encouragement and support for yourself that you should note? Is He asking you to encourage or support someone in particular? Is He showing you an adjustment you need to make in your life? Have you seen answered prayers? Write these things down so you create a record of God's goodness to you.

Day 18

Praying with Faith

Pray: "Lord, show me how a shield of faith works for me."

Scripture: Habakkuk 2:2-4

Write the vision; make it plain on tablets, so he may run who reads it. ³For still the vision awaits its appointed time; it hastens to the end—it will not lie. If it seems slow, wait for it; it will surely come; it will not delay. ⁴ "Behold, his soul is puffed up; it is not upright within him, but the righteous shall live by his faith.

Scripture: John 1:1-17

In the beginning was the Word, and the Word was with God, and the Word was God. ² He was in the beginning with God. ³ All things were made through him, and without him was not any thing made that was made. ⁴ In him was life, and the life was the light of men. ⁵ The light shines in the darkness, and the darkness has not overcome it. ⁶ There was a man sent from God, whose name was John. ⁷He came as a witness, to bear witness about the light, that all might believe through him. ⁸ He was not the light, but came to bear witness about the light. ⁹ The true light, which gives light to everyone, was coming into the world. ¹⁰ He was in the world, and the world was made through him, yet the world did not know him. ¹¹ He came to his own, and his own people did not receive him. ¹² But to all who did receive him, who believed in his name, he gave the right to become children of God, ¹³ who were born, not of blood nor of the will of the flesh nor of the will of man, but of God.

¹⁴ And the Word became flesh and dwelt among us, and we have seen his glory, glory as of the only Son from the Father, full of grace and truth. ¹⁵ (John bore witness about him, and cried out, "This was he of whom I said, 'He who comes after me ranks before me, because he was before me.'") ¹⁶ For from his fullness we have all received, grace upon grace. ¹⁷ For the law was given through Moses; grace and truth came through Jesus Christ. ¹⁸ No one has ever seen God; the only God, who is at the Father's side, he has made him known.

Day 18: Praying with Faith

"...above all, taking the shield of faith with which, you will be able to quench all the fiery darts of the wicked one." Ephesians 6:16

Fiery darts can come in many shapes and sizes. They can come pounding and fast in the form of fear, doubt, and guilt. They can sneak in from the side as habits, misinformation, and negative thoughts. Faith is our weapon to quench the darts so that they don't threaten our walk with Christ.

Now faith is the substance of things hoped for, the evidence of things not seen. Hebrews 11:1

Our faith is what we expectantly hope for, our assurance in Jesus. Notice in Ephesians 6:16 that faith isn't something that we put on, it is a shield that we actively use. We thrust it out in front to protect us from the darts coming our way.

"I have been crucified with Christ; it is no longer I who live but Christ lives in me; and the life which I now live in the flesh I live by faith in the Son of God who loved me and gave Himself for me." Galatians 2:20

Paul wrote the letter of Galatians. His faith was constantly growing and challenged. He strengthened his shield of faith by knowing the Word of God, by spending time talking with Christ, and through experiences. He was persecuted, in prison, traveling, and writing. Through all these things he kept seeing God's faithfulness, which increased his own faith and helped him anticipate darts.

The Roman foot soldier carried his shield that protected him from darts and arrows as he knelt behind it. Kneeling is the posture that uses our faith to protect us from our enemy's darts and arrows.

Prayer:
Dear Father, I am excited to fight with the shield of faith. Help me see fiery darts coming so I can use my faith in You to battle. Increase my faith. Use your Word, circumstances, and my relationship with you to grow me closer to you. Grow my faith in who You are and in what You have done for me so I can accept and enjoy your grace and goodness more completely. Let my faith be the kind that makes myself and others whole. In Jesus name, Amen.

Continue writing your prayer here:

Day 18: Praying with Faith

1. What fiery darts threaten you that you can combat with faith?

2. What is one way you can grow in your faith today?

3. Who do you admire that is full of faith? Why do they have strong faith?

Day 18: JOURNAL

Take a few moments to stop and LISTEN to the Lord; then write down what you sense He is telling you. Is He giving you words of encouragement and support for yourself that you should note? Is He asking you to encourage or support someone in particular? Is He showing you an adjustment you need to make in your life? Have you seen answered prayers? Write these things down so you create a record of God's goodness to you.

Day 19

Salvation and Prayer

Pray: "Lord, thank you for paying the price for my salvation."

Scripture: Acts 16:25-40

About midnight Paul and Silas were praying and singing hymns to God, and the prisoners were listening to them, 26 and suddenly there was a great earthquake, so that the foundations of the prison were shaken. And immediately all the doors were opened, and everyone's bonds were unfastened. 27 When the jailer woke and saw that the prison doors were open, he drew his sword and was about to kill himself, supposing that the prisoners had escaped. 28 But Paul cried with a loud voice, "Do not harm yourself, for we are all here." 29 And the jailer called for lights and rushed in, and trembling with fear he fell down before Paul and Silas. 30 Then he brought them out and said, "Sirs, what must I do to be saved?" 31 And they said, "Believe in the Lord Jesus, and you will be saved, you and your household." 32 And they spoke the word of the Lord to him and to all who were in his house. 33 And he took them the same hour of the night and washed their wounds; and he was baptized at once, he and all his family. 34 Then he brought them up into his house and set food before them. And he rejoiced along with his entire household that he had believed in God. 35 But when it was day, the magistrates sent the police, saying, "the magistrates sent the police, saying, "Let those men go." ³⁶ And the jailer reported these words to Paul, saying, "The magistrates have sent to let you go. Therefore, come out now and go in peace." ³⁷ But Paul said to them, "They have beaten us publicly, uncondemned men who are Roman citizens, and have thrown us into prison; and do they now throw us out secretly? No! Let them come themselves and take us out." ³⁸ The police reported these words to the magistrates, and they were afraid when they heard that they were Roman citizens. ³⁹ So they came and apologized to them. And they took them out and asked them to leave the city. ⁴⁰ So they went out of the prison and visited Lydia. And when they had seen the brothers, they encouraged them and departed.

Day 19: Salvation and Prayer

"...and take the helmet of salvation..." Ephesians 6:17

There is power in salvation. Salvation is not something that we can do on our own, but we can fight in Jesus' name because of being given salvation. When we are covered in His blood, forgiven and pure, we cannot be condemned by the Enemy.

For I am not ashamed of the gospel of Christ, for it is the power of God to salvation for everyone who believes, for the Jew first and also for the Greek." Romans 1:16

Salvation is the starting point of our journey. It is believing that Jesus Christ died for our sins, accepting Him, being forgiven, and committing our lives to Him. It is what secures us eternally. *But even with* being secure eternally, we still have battles to fight and a relationship with God to strengthen while we are on this earth.

"Not that I have already attained, or am already perfected; but I press on, that I may lay hold of that for which Christ Jesus has also laid hold of me." Philippians 3:12

We can press on and do all we can to get salvation and yet it cannot be earned. We can only accept it. It's been done because of God's great mercy (we don't get what we deserve) and grace (we get something incredibly good that we don't deserve).

Titus 3:4-7 **4** *But when the goodness and loving kindness of God our Savior appeared,* **5** *he saved us, not because of works done by us in righteousness, but according to his own mercy, by the washing of regeneration and renewal of the Holy Spirit,* **6** *whom he poured out on us richly through Jesus Christ our Savior,* **7** *so that being justified by his grace we might become heirs according to the hope of eternal life.*

Prayer:

Lord, thank you for bringing me to you, for forgiving me and giving me a helmet of salvation to wear. You have equipped me to fight. Thank you for giving me not only salvation, but a purpose and tools to accomplish what you set in front of me. Give me the opportunity to share this great gift with others. In Jesus name, Amen.

Continue writing your prayer here:

Day 19: Salvation and Prayer

1. Describe your encounter with Christ, when He gave you salvation:

2. Why is salvation significant in our battle; as part of our armor?

3. Who would you most like to see receive salvation? After writing their name/s down pray specifically for them.

Day 19: JOURNAL

Take a few moments to stop and LISTEN to the Lord; then write down what you sense He is telling you. Is He giving you words of encouragement and support for yourself that you should note? Is He asking you to encourage or support someone in particular? Is He showing you an adjustment you need to make in your life? Have you seen answered prayers? Write these things down so you create a record of God's goodness to you.

Day 20

Wielding a Sword

Pray: "Lord, show me how to use Your word in my prayers."

Scripture: Hebrews 4:1-13

Therefore, while the promise of entering his rest still stands, let us fear lest any of you should seem to have failed to reach it. ² For good news came to us just as to them, but the message they heard did not benefit them, because they were not united by faith with those who listened. ³ For we who have believed enter that rest, as he has said,
"As I swore in my wrath, 'They shall not enter my rest,'"
although his works were finished from the foundation of the world. ⁴ For he has somewhere spoken of the seventh day in this way: "And God rested on the seventh day from all his works." ⁵ And again in this passage he said,
"They shall not enter my rest."
⁶ Since therefore it remains for some to enter it, and those who formerly received the good news failed to enter because of disobedience, ⁷ again he appoints a certain day, "Today," saying through David so long afterward, in the words already quoted,
"Today, if you hear his voice, do not harden your hearts."
⁸ For if Joshua had given them rest, God would not have spoken of another day later on. ⁹ So then, there remains a Sabbath rest for the people of God, ¹⁰ for whoever has

entered God's rest has also rested from his works as God did from his.

[11] Let us therefore strive to enter that rest, so that no one may fall by the same sort of disobedience. [12] For the word of God is living and active, sharper than any two-edged sword, piercing to the division of soul and of spirit, of joints and of marrow, and discerning the thoughts and intentions of the heart. [13] And no creature is hidden from his sight, but all are naked and exposed to the eyes of him to whom we must give account.

Day 20: Wielding a Sword

"...and the sword of the Spirit, which is the word of God;"

It is not enough to carry a sword around. You must know how to use it. A sword might look powerful and intimidating, but it has no practical use unless you know how to handle it and apply it in battle.

For the word of God is living and powerful, and sharper than any two-edged sword, piercing even to the division of soul and spirit, and of joints and marrow, and is a discerner of the thoughts and intents of the heart. Hebrews 4:12

It is not enough to read a verse a day for inspiration. It's not enough to know a bunch of facts or be able to win a game of Bible Trivia. Knowing the Word of God means to meditate on it, to mull it over, to know how to use it in spiritual battle.

"Your word is a lamp to my feet and a light to my path." Psalm 119:105

We can commit our lives to God, have our salvation secure, and still have an unstable, tumultuous life. We don't know God's power, our purpose, or answers if we don't know God's Word.

As you read the Bible, ask God to show you how specific Scripture applies to your life. Memorize it! Post verses in places where you can meditate on it; the bathroom mirror, the steering wheel of your car, on the refrigerator, or on your phone.

Did you notice that what you read in Hebrews seems to be more about "rest" in God than anything else? That rest is entered into through the word of God and letting it saturate your life.

Prayer:
Lord Jesus I'm asking that by the power of the Holy Spirit in me I would continue to grow in Your word. Show me what You might want me to memorize. Show me how, where, and when to share Your amazing word with others. Allow me to rest in You as Your word rests in me. Let me continue to increase in my knowledge and love of You. In Jesus name, Amen.

Continue writing your prayer here:

Day 20: Wielding a Sword

1. What are you doing to know the Bible?

2. Ask God what He wants you to do with His Word. Write down what you sense He is saying to you:

3. What will you do this week to apply something you have learned?

Day 20: JOURNAL

Take a few moments to stop and LISTEN to the Lord; then write down what you sense He is telling you. Is He giving you words of encouragement and support for yourself that you should note? Is He asking you to encourage or support someone in particular? Is He showing you an adjustment you need to make in your life? Have you seen answered prayers? Write these things down so you create a record of God's goodness to you.

Day 21

Armor Reflection

Pray: "Lord, let me give you praise in every way You show me."

Scripture: Psalm 47

Clap your hands, all peoples!
    Shout to God with loud songs of joy!
2 For the LORD, the Most High, is to be feared,
    a great king over all the earth.
3 He subdued peoples under us,
    and nations under our feet.
4 He chose our heritage for us,
    the pride of Jacob whom he loves. *Selah*

5 God has gone up with a shout,
    the LORD with the sound of a trumpet.
6 Sing praises to God, sing praises!
    Sing praises to our King, sing praises!
7 For God is the King of all the earth;
    sing praises with a psalm!

8 God reigns over the nations;
    God sits on his holy throne.
9 The princes of the peoples gather
    as the people of the God of Abraham.
    For the shields of the earth belong to God;
    he is highly exalted!

Day 21: Armor Reflection

God has given us all kinds of ways that He wants us to bring Him praise and to connect and communicate with Him. Psalm 47 begins by telling us to literally clap our hands for Him. And then He lets us know that even the rivers do that: *Psalm 98:8 [8] Let the rivers clap their hands; let the hills sing for joy together...*

Not only are we called to clap, but we are also told to shout! I get the sense that this is almost like a battle shout. We get to shout out to the Lord and then it says He has gone up with a shout. Somehow that shout of ours moves God in the spiritual realm and carries with it the sound of trumpets. He is going to war on our behalf, and He is the King over all the earth!

So, we clap, shout and sing. Sometimes we can combine all three at one time. I enjoy doing this in my truck or on my motorcycle, while driving. Being by myself, picturing Jesus in the seat next to me and singing to Him at the top of my lungs is not only fun - it's scriptural! Admittedly you may have people driving next to you wondering what you are doing but that's just another fun part of the experience. I'm relieved that when I sing to Him, He never judges me for quality of voice or if I happen to be in the right key or not.

"May we shout for joy over your salvation, and in the name of our God set up our banners! May the Lord fulfill all your petitions!" Psalm 20:5

Prayer:

Lord Jesus, I want to honor you in the way I bring praise to You. So, I'm going to clap for you, shout for you and sing to you because You've asked me to. Help me get over my fear and/or embarrassment so that it doesn't get in the way of giving You what You deserve... and that's everything I have and all that I am. When I stop and think about what You have done for me and the way You have loved me, I'm overwhelmed with gratitude. Accept my gratitude today. In Jesus name, Amen.

Continue writing your prayer here:

Day 21: Armor Reflection

Look over the last 6 days of devotions.

1. What new things have you learned this past week?

2. How has God spoken to you in the past week?

3. What have you learned or prayed about that you can practically apply to your life?

Day 21: JOURNAL

Ask God now if there is more, He wants to show you or say to you. Spend time quietly waiting for Him to move in you until something specific speaks to you. Write about it here:

Day 22

The Impact of Prayerlessness

Pray: "Lord, remind me to keep you in the front of my mind."

Scripture: James 1:1-18

James, a servant of God and of the Lord Jesus Christ,

To the twelve tribes in the Dispersion:

Greetings.

² Count it all joy, my brothers, when you meet trials of various kinds, ³ for you know that the testing of your faith produces steadfastness. ⁴ And let steadfastness have its full effect, that you may be perfect and complete, lacking in nothing.

⁵ If any of you lacks wisdom, let him ask God, who gives generously to all without reproach, and it will be given him. ⁶ But let him ask in faith, with no doubting, for the one who doubts is like a wave of the sea that is driven and tossed by the wind. ⁷ For that person must not suppose that he will receive anything from the Lord; ⁸ he is a double-minded man, unstable in all his ways.

⁹ Let the lowly brother boast in his exaltation, ¹⁰ and the rich in his humiliation, because like a flower of the grass he will pass away. ¹¹ For the sun rises with its scorching heat and withers the grass; its flower falls, and its beauty perishes. So also, will the rich man fade away in the midst of his pursuits.

¹² Blessed is the man who remains steadfast under trial, for when he has stood the test he will receive the crown of life, which God has promised to those who love him. ¹³ Let no one say when he is tempted, "I am being tempted by God," for God cannot be tempted with evil, and he himself tempts no one. ¹⁴ But each person is tempted when he is lured and enticed by his own desire. ¹⁵ Then desire when it has conceived gives birth to sin, and sin when it is fully grown brings forth death.

¹⁶ Do not be deceived, my beloved brothers. ¹⁷ Every good gift and every perfect gift is from above, coming down from the Father of lights, with whom there is no variation or shadow due to change. ¹⁸ Of his own will he brought us forth by the word of truth, that we should be a kind of first fruits of his creatures.

Day 22: The Impact of Prayerlessness

Therefore, submit to God. Resist the devil and he will flee from you. Draw near to God and He will draw near to you.
James 4:7,8a

We start to feel disconnected in our relationship with God when we aren't praying consistently. A person can't expect to stay close to someone and grow in relationship if they aren't communicating and having quality time together.

What does 'drawing near' to God look like?* How do you conquer prayerlessness? We should be training ourselves so that prayer is our first reaction to everything. If something unexpected comes up- pray. If something exciting happens- praise and pray. If something hurtful happens- pray.

As a starting place, read Matthew 11:28, *"Come to Me, all you who labor and are heavy laden, and I will give you rest."* First, go to Christ with everything resting on your shoulders. Picture taking them off your shoulders and handing them to Jesus so He can carry them for you. You might want to actually carry out the motions to make it easier to imagine the transaction. Then do as Mary did and enjoy the time with Him.

"And she had a sister called Mary, who also sat at Jesus' feet and heard His Word." Luke 10:39

Relationships are built with time. Don't be discouraged, simply use today as a place to start making prayer your first reaction. Today find a place where you can sit and hear God's Word. Bring your burdens and stay long enough to listen. Start by telling Him out loud what you are dealing with on the inside and then you can work outward to what you are experiencing on the outside.

Prayer:

Lord, I don't want to put you on the back burner of my life. I'm sorry for not always coming to you as my first reaction. I come to you now with everything, knowing you can give me rest. Please speak to my heart as I listen to you.

Write anything you want to remember from this prayer time:

Day 22: The Impact of Prayerlessness

1. Have you ever felt disconnected in your relationship with God? Write about it here:

2. What would you want your prayer times to look like?

3. What do you need to do to achieve better times of prayer?

Day 22: JOURNAL

Take a few moments to stop and LISTEN to the Lord; then write down what you sense He is telling you. Is He giving you words of encouragement and support for yourself that you should note? Is He asking you to encourage or support someone in particular? Is He showing you an adjustment you need to make in your life? Have you seen answered prayers? Write these things down so you create a record of God's goodness to you.

Day 23

The Roadblock of Unconfessed Sin

Pray: "Lord, if there are sins I need to confess please show me."

Scripture: James 4:1-12

What causes quarrels and what causes fights among you? Is it not this, that your passions are at war within you? [2] You desire and do not have, so you murder. You covet and cannot obtain, so you fight and quarrel. You do not have, because you do not ask. [3] You ask and do not receive, because you ask wrongly, to spend it on your passions. [4] You adulterous people! Do you not know that friendship with the world is enmity with God?

Therefore, whoever wishes to be a friend of the world makes himself an enemy of God. [5] Or do you suppose it is to no purpose that the Scripture says, "He yearns jealously over the spirit that he has made to dwell in us"? [6] But he gives more grace.

Therefore, it says, "God opposes the proud but gives grace to the humble." [7] Submit yourselves therefore to God. Resist the devil, and he will flee from you. [8] Draw near to God, and he will draw near to you. Cleanse your hands, you sinners, and purify your hearts, you double-minded. [9] Be wretched and mourn and weep. Let your laughter be turned to mourning and your joy to gloom. [10] Humble yourselves before the Lord, and he will exalt you.

¹¹ Do not speak evil against one another, brothers. The one who speaks against a brother or judges his brother, speaks evil against the law and judges the law. But if you judge the law, you are not a doer of the law but a judge. ¹² There is only one lawgiver and judge, he who is able to save and to destroy. But who are you to judge your neighbor?

Proverbs 28:13-14
Whoever conceals his transgressions will not prosper, but he who confesses and forsakes them will obtain mercy.
¹⁴ Blessed is the one who fears the LORD always, but whoever hardens his heart will fall into calamity.

Day 23: The Roadblock of Unconfessed Sin

I John 1:8-10 ⁸If we say we have no sin, we deceive ourselves, and the truth is not in us. ⁹ If we confess our sins, he is faithful and just to forgive us our sins and to cleanse us from all unrighteousness. ¹⁰ If we say we have not sinned, we make him a liar, and his word is not in us.

Yesterday we read about drawing near to God. The next part of the Scripture in James is this; getting sin out.

We let sin go unconfessed in our lives for a number of reasons. Sometimes we don't confess because we know deep down we intend to do the same thing again. We are often hard hearted and don't see the sin in our lives. We don't slow down long enough to evaluate and ask forgiveness. We are afraid. We try to justify what we've done or intentionally hide it. We compartmentalize our lives and only let God have certain aspects, letting other areas go unchecked. We worry that maybe we've blown it so big that God can't forgive this time.

Regardless of the reason, unconfessed sin eats away at us and comes between us and Jesus. It is a roadblock that needs to be removed.

If you have been frustrated, feeling like you can't break through in your relationship with God, ask Him to reveal any unconfessed sin in your life. He *will* forgive you and *wants* to forgive you. He has not given up on you and will answer when you come to Him.

I John 1:9 *"If we confess our sins, He is faithful and just to forgive our sins and to cleanse us from all unrighteousness."*

Prayer:

Walk through James 4:8-10 right now.

Cleanse your hands and purify your hearts: Tell God you don't want to please yourself and Him, you want to just please Him. Ask Him to forgive you. You can't cleanse your hands on your own.

Lament and mourn and weep: Share your anguish at having unconfessed sin in your life. Know that sin breaks the Lord's heart, and it should break yours too.

Humble yourselves and He will lift you up: When you are forgiven, God will give you grace (you haven't earned it, you just asked for it) and He will heal and encourage you.

Continue writing your prayer here:

Day 23: The Roadblock of Unconfessed Sin

1. Is there sin coming between you and the Lord? If so, what is it?

2. Confess your sin to God. And thank Him for forgiving you. Write down here what you would like God to do for you to overcome this sin and what you will do to see it overcome.

3. Why do you think unconfessed sin can get between us and having our prayers heard and answered?

Day 23: JOURNAL

Take a few moments to stop and LISTEN to the Lord; then write down what you sense He is telling you. Is He giving you words of encouragement and support for yourself that you should note? Is He asking you to encourage or support someone in particular? Is He showing you an adjustment you need to make in your life? Have you seen answered prayers? Write these things down so you create a record of God's goodness to you.

Day 24

Compelling Confessions

Pray: "Lord, give me the honesty and boldness to confess to others."

Scripture: Isaiah 59 – Excerpts

Behold, the LORD's hand is not shortened, that it cannot save,
    or his ear dull, that it cannot hear;
2 but your iniquities have made a separation
    between you and your God,
and your sins have hidden his face from you
    so that he does not hear.
3 For your hands are defiled with blood
    and your fingers with iniquity;
your lips have spoken lies;
    your tongue mutters wickedness.
4 No one enters suit justly;
    no one goes to law honestly;
they rely on empty pleas, they speak lies,
    they conceive mischief and give birth to iniquity…
14 Justice is turned back,
    and righteousness stands far away;
for truth has stumbled in the public squares,
    and uprightness cannot enter.
15 Truth is lacking,

>   and he who departs from evil makes himself a
>   prey...
> ²⁰ "And a Redeemer will come to Zion,
>   to those in Jacob who turn from transgression,"
>   declares the L<small>ORD</small>.
> ²¹ "And as for me, this is my covenant with them," says the L<small>ORD</small>: "My Spirit that is upon you, and my words that I have put in your mouth, shall not depart out of your mouth, or out of the mouth of your offspring, or out of the mouth of your children's offspring," says the L<small>ORD</small>, "from this time forth and forevermore."

Day 24: Compelling Confessions

Sometimes it's hard to confess our sins to God. I must remind myself that He already knows all my sins and even those I'm not aware of. I also remind myself that He died to pay the price of my sins, while I was still a sinner – didn't even know or acknowledge Him! So, I can trust His love and His confidence. But then He tells us to confess to others as well! That's a lot harder for me. But He tells us to do it and guarantees benefits when we do.

Confess your trespasses to one another, and pray for one another, that you may be healed. The effective, fervent prayer of a righteous man avails much. James 5:16b

God didn't design us to do everything on our own. Not only does He give us His strength to do what is otherwise impossible, He also gives us the Body of Christ, other believers. It's easy to shut ourselves off to being vulnerable or open with other people. It can be very challenging to be completely and consistently honest about where we are in our walk with Christ. James speaks about the importance of having someone to confess to and pray with. Our salvation and forgiveness do not hinge on confessing to other people, but we are able to grow in ways we can't on our own.

Be receptive to other people's perceptions. Don't be defensive. If you are approached, be willing to do some self-examination. Ask for input from godly people you trust. Understand that humans are imperfect but can still contribute and encourage our walks with Christ. If you don't have anyone with whom you can share on a deep level pray that God will send someone your way. Begin by approaching other people acting as the type of person you would want to trust with your "stuff".

Prayer:

Lord, give me the courage to confess the way You want me to so that my prayers are effective and that they will accomplish much for You and Your kingdom. In Jesus name, Amen.

Continue writing your prayer here:

Day 24: Compelling Confessions

1. Who do you trust that you confess things in your life to?

2. Write your prayer down today. If you don't have someone you confess to and pray with, ask God to open your eyes to someone.

3. Why do you think confession is good for the heart and soul?

Day 24: JOURNAL

Take a few moments to stop and LISTEN to the Lord; then write down what you sense He is telling you. Is He giving you words of encouragement and support for yourself that you should note? Is He asking you to encourage or support someone in particular? Is He showing you an adjustment you need to make in your life? Have you seen answered prayers? Write these things down so you create a record of God's goodness to you.

Day 25

Roadblock - Broken Relationships

Pray: "Lord, heal broken relationships so my prayers are heard."

Scripture: Matthew 18:15-35 - Excerpts

"If your brother sins against you, go and tell him his fault, between you and him alone. If he listens to you, you have gained your brother. ¹⁶ But if he does not listen, take one or two others along with you, that every charge may be established by the evidence of two or three witnesses. ¹⁷ If he refuses to listen to them, tell it to the church. And if he refuses to listen even to the church, let him be to you as a Gentile and a tax collector... ²¹ Then Peter came up and said to him, "Lord, how often will my brother sin against me, and I forgive him? As many as seven times?" ²² Jesus said to him, "I do not say to you seven times, but seventy-seven times.

²³ "Therefore the kingdom of heaven may be compared to a king who wished to settle accounts with his servants. ²⁴ When he began to settle, one was brought to him who owed him ten thousand talents. ²⁵ And since he could not pay, his master ordered him to be sold, with his wife and children and all that he had, and payment to be made. ²⁶ So the servant fell on his knees, imploring him, 'Have patience with me, and I will pay you everything.' ²⁷ And out of pity for him, the master of that servant released him and forgave him the debt. ²⁸ But when that same servant went

out, he found one of his fellow servants who owed him a hundred denarii, and seizing him, he began to choke him, saying, 'Pay what you owe.' ²⁹ So his fellow servant fell down and pleaded with him, 'Have patience with me, and I will pay you.' ³⁰ He refused and went and put him in prison until he should pay the debt. ³¹ When his fellow servants saw what had taken place, they were greatly distressed, and they went and reported to their master all that had taken place. ³² Then his master summoned him and said to him, 'You wicked servant! I forgave you all that debt because you pleaded with me. ³³ And should not you have had mercy on your fellow servant, as I had mercy on you?' ³⁴ And in anger his master delivered him to the jailers, until he should pay all his debt. ³⁵ So also my heavenly Father will do to every one of you, if you do not forgive your brother from your heart."

Day 25: Roadblock - Broken Relationships

Therefore, if you bring your gift to the altar, and there remember that your brother has something against you, leave your gift there before the altar and go your way. First be reconciled to your brother, and then come and offer your gift. Matthew 5:23,24

God does not even want your gift, or sacrifice, until you have made your relationships right. He requires us to extend the same grace and forgiveness that He gives freely to us. It is by our love and relationships, that people will see Christ.

Pursue peace with all people and holiness, without which no one will see the Lord; looking carefully lest anyone fall short of the grace of God; lest any root of bitterness springing up cause trouble, and by this many become defiled; Hebrews 12:14,15

Healing broken relationships is hard. Sometimes it means repeatedly making it right; forgiving over and over when someone doesn't even deserve it or apologizing over and over when we continue hurting someone.

When making a relationship right before God, first pray. God's power will do what feels impossible. Sometimes we have to choose to forgive before the feeling is there. Pray first for the person, then for your relationship with that person. Ask God to show you how He views them and the situation. Getting a relationship right might mean going to the person, or it might require keeping it between you and God; it's your heart God is working in. Ask Him to discern for you.

Prayer:
Lord, I pray for _____. Show me how to see_____ through your perspective. Give me your love to extend. Please be in our relationship and reconciliation as I _____.
Give me the words, the grace, the healing that needs to happen. Thank you, for giving me relationships and people that are important to you. Amen.

Continue writing your prayer here:

Day 25: Roadblock - Broken Relationships

1. Is God bringing to mind a relationship you need to make right?

2. How do the benefits of doing this hard thing, (asking and giving forgiveness), outweigh holding on to the hurt?

3. How will you forgive or ask forgiveness?

Now...take action!

Day 25: JOURNAL

Take a few moments to stop and LISTEN to the Lord; then write down what you sense He is telling you. Is He giving you words of encouragement and support for yourself that you should note? Is He asking you to encourage or support someone in particular? Is He showing you an adjustment you need to make in your life? Have you seen answered prayers? Write these things down so you create a record of God's goodness to you.

Day 26

The Roadblock of Selfishness

Pray: "Lord, show me if selfishness is impeding my prayers."

Scripture: 2 Kings 5:14-27 - Excerpts

So Naaman went down and dipped himself seven times in the Jordan, according to the word of the man of God, and his flesh was restored like the flesh of a little child, and he was clean. [15] Then he returned to the man of God, he and all his company, and he came and stood before him. And he said, "Behold, I know that there is no God in all the earth but in Israel; so accept now a present from your servant." [16] But he said, "As the LORD lives, before whom I stand, I will receive none." And he urged him to take it, but he refused...

But when Naaman had gone from him a short distance, [20] Gehazi, the servant of Elisha the man of God, said, "See, my master has spared this Naaman the Syrian, in not accepting from his hand what he brought. As the LORD lives, I will run after him and get something from him." [21] So Gehazi followed Naaman. And when Naaman saw someone running after him, he got down from the chariot to meet him and said, "Is all well?" [22] And he said, "All is well. My master has sent me to say, 'There have just now come to me from the hill country of Ephraim two young men of the sons of the prophets. Please give them a talent of silver and two changes of clothing.'"

²³ And Naaman said, "Be pleased to accept two talents." And he urged him and tied up two talents of silver in two bags, with two changes of clothing, and laid them on two of his servants. And they carried them before Gehazi. ²⁴ And when he came to the hill, he took them from their hand and put them in the house, and he sent the men away, and they departed. ²⁵ He went in and stood before his master, and Elisha said to him, "Where have you been, Gehazi?" And he said, "Your servant went nowhere." ²⁶ But he said to him, "Did not my heart go when the man turned from his chariot to meet you? Was it a time to accept money and garments, olive orchards and vineyards, sheep and oxen, male servants, and female servants? ²⁷ Therefore the leprosy of Naaman shall cling to you and to your descendants forever."

Day 26: The Roadblock of Selfishness

Whoever shuts his ears to the cry of the poor will also cry himself and not be heard. Proverbs 21:13

It's so easy to do and so hard not to do. Easy to ignore others and so hard not to put ourselves above anyone else. Selfishness is a disease everyone struggles with, and it can be something that negatively impacts our prayers and our prayer life.

Where do your treasures (your time, money, talents, relationships) lie? *For where your treasure is, there your heart will be also. Matthew 6:21*

Selfishness is hard to root out because it sneaks in, in many forms. We often see the results of selfishness in the way we guard our time, what we spend money on, or the way we use what God has given us.

What do you say is most important in your life? Does your time reflect that? Your money? The way you use your talents? Your relationships?

We might do all the "right" "noble" things; volunteer, tithe, participate in worthwhile events, and still lack love. Even if we go through the right motions, if our motive and ultimate desire is self-gratification and self-love, we are performing out of selfishness, not the love and grace of Christ.

To love others with the love of Christ, we must first experience His love. If we don't truly believe we're forgiven and unconditionally loved, we'll have a hard time extending it to others. If we have been set free and are being transformed by the renewing of our mind, we will begin to set aside selfishness for the furtherance of God's kingdom.

Prayer:

Lord, Expose any selfishness in me. Show me your love and grace so that it is foremost in my mind and heart. May it drive out self-love so that all that remains is love for you. I don't want anything to come between us, God. Make me sensitive to you. In Jesus name, Amen.

Continue writing your prayer here:

Day 26: The Roadblock of Selfishness

1. Would you say your priorities line up with your actions? How?

2. In what areas of your life does selfishness rear its ugly head?

3. How can you prevent selfishness from becoming a roadblock in your relationship with the Lord?

Day 26: JOURNAL

Take a few moments to stop and LISTEN to the Lord; then write down what you sense He is telling you. Is He giving you words of encouragement and support for yourself that you should note? Is He asking you to encourage or support someone in particular? Is He showing you an adjustment you need to make in your life? Have you seen answered prayers? Write these things down so you create a record of God's goodness to you.

Day 27

The Value of Faithful Prayers

Pray: "Lord, increase my faith so I can please You more."

Scripture: Hebrews 11 – Excerpts

Now faith is the assurance of things hoped for, the conviction of things not seen. ² For by it the people of old received their commendation. ³ By faith we understand that the universe was created by the Word of God, so that what is seen was not made out of things that are visible.

⁴ By faith Abel offered to God a more acceptable sacrifice than Cain, through which he was commended as righteous, God commending him by accepting his gifts. And through his faith, though he died, he still speaks. ⁵ By faith Enoch was taken up so that he should not see death, and he was not found, because God had taken him. Now before he was taken, he was commended as having pleased God. ⁶ And without faith it is impossible to please him, for whoever would draw near to God must believe that he exists and that he rewards those who seek him. ⁷ By faith Noah, being warned by God concerning events as yet unseen, in reverent fear constructed an ark for the saving of his household. By this he condemned the world and became an heir of the righteousness that comes by faith...

¹³ These all died in faith, not having received the things promised, but having seen them and greeted them from afar, and having acknowledged that they were strangers

and exiles on the earth. ¹⁴ For people who speak thus make it clear that they are seeking a homeland. ¹⁵ If they had been thinking of that land from which they had gone out, they would have had opportunity to return. ¹⁶ But as it is, they desire a better country, that is, a heavenly one. Therefore God is not ashamed to be called their God, for he has prepared for them a city...

³⁹ And all these, though commended through their faith, did not receive what was promised, ⁴⁰ since God had provided something better for us, that apart from us they should not be made perfect.

Day 27: The Value of Faithful Prayers

If any of you lacks wisdom, let him ask of God, who gives to all liberally and without reproach, and it will be given to him. But let him ask in faith, with no doubting, for he who doubts is like a wave of the sea driven and tossed by the wind. For let not that man suppose that he will receive anything from the Lord; he is a double-minded man, unstable in all his ways. James 1:5-8

If you feel that your faith is inadequate, that you struggle asking without doubting, ask God for wisdom as verse 5 says. Ask God to increase your faith.

In Hebrews 11 we are reminded of people in the Old Testament who had great faith. They weren't people without fault, and some of them had moments of doubt. But as their understanding of God grew, so did their faith. They learned to pray in accordance with His will as they knew Him more. *Therefore, do not cast away your confidence, which has great reward. Hebrews 10:35*

They were determined to believe even if they could not see the reason to and God honored them for that and points them out as examples of great faith for us.

To strengthen your faith, make a record of times God has already proven Himself faithful in your life. Use a journal to write things down, list answers to prayers you've received. In the Old Testament people often built memorials of stones to remind them of something God had done. Build a memorial in your backyard, share your testimony, do something to remember.

Prayer:
Dear God, you say to ask for wisdom, and you will give liberally. I ask that you give me wisdom and increase my faith. Lord, I believe without doubting that you will build my faith in you. I trust you and know that you are worthy of my confidence. In Jesus name, Amen.

Continue writing your prayer here:

Day 27: The Value of Faithful Prayers

1. What has God done to show Himself faithful?

2. How can you celebrate and remember it?

3. What would you most like faith to do?

Day 27: JOURNAL

Take a few moments to stop and LISTEN to the Lord; then write down what you sense He is telling you. Is He giving you words of encouragement and support for yourself that you should note? Is He asking you to encourage or support someone in particular? Is He showing you an adjustment you need to make in your life? Have you seen answered prayers? Write these things down so you create a record of God's goodness to you.

Day 28

Restful Prayers

Pray: "Lord, let me rest in Your goodness and with Your words."

Scripture: Psalm 4

Answer me when I call, O God of my righteousness!
   You have given me relief when I was in distress.
   Be gracious to me and hear my prayer!
2 O men, how long shall my honor be turned into shame?
   How long will you love vain words and seek after lies? *Selah*
3 But know that the LORD has set apart the godly for himself;
   the LORD hears when I call to him. ⁴ Be angry, and do not sin; ponder in your own hearts on your beds, and be silent. *Selah*
5 Offer right sacrifices, and put your trust in the LORD.
6 There are many who say, "Who will show us some good?
   Lift up the light of your face upon us, O LORD!"
7 You have put more joy in my heart
   than they have when their grain and wine abound.
8 In peace I will both lie down and sleep;
   for you alone, O LORD, make me dwell in safety.

Day 28: Restful Prayers

The idea of "Selah," is a pause. A time of reflection and to think about what was just read, sung, or spoken. The Psalmist encourages us to take a selah to better understand, meditate on and absorb the word of God.

This is the day for you to take a selah and rest before God so that you will better understand Him, enjoy Him, and come to know Him and His wonderful character.

The Psalms are full of instances of praying to God, praising God, and calling on God. They make it very clear that we should be calling on God, (praying) when we are in trouble, when we are doing great and when we are experiencing the everyday normalcy of life.

Most of us have no problem praying passionately when things are difficult, when we don't know what to do and when life is out of control for us. But it's a different thing when all is well, and we don't seem to have a need for God. How sad that we could and often are such fickle lovers of the One who saved our souls and paid the price for our sins.

Today, commit again to put your trust in the Lord. Take time to thank Him that He doesn't treat us like we treat Him. Share with someone else a testimony of things God has shown you, prayers He has answered for you or what you are asking Him to do for you… or them! And then call on the Lord, "who is worthy to be praised!"

Prayer:

Lord Jesus, You are worthy to be praised. You hear me when I am in distress and trouble. You hear me when things are going well. You take the time to hear me, and You care for me. Show me how to make my prayers less about me and more about what You want me to pray. Forgive me when my prayers are so much about myself and my circumstances that I forget to pray the way You want me to and for the people and circumstances that You want me to pray for. Lord, I want to see answers to prayers that will give a testimony to Your goodness and love. I commit to share Your goodness with others as I see it in my life. In Jesus name, Amen.

Continue writing your prayer here:

Day 28: Restful Prayers

Look over the last six days of devotions

1. What have you learned about roadblocks in your prayer life?

2. How has this week affected your prayer life?

3. What have you specifically shared with others about God's goodness to you?

Day 28: JOURNAL

Take a few moments to stop and LISTEN to the Lord; then write down what you sense He is telling you. Is He giving you words of encouragement and support for yourself that you should note? Is He asking you to encourage or support someone in particular? Is He showing you an adjustment you need to make in your life? Have you seen answered prayers? Write these things down so you create a record of God's goodness to you.

Day 29

Is it His Will?

Pray: *"Lord, let my prayers be prayers of Your will for me."*

Scripture: Psalm 28

To you, O LORD, I call;
    my rock, be not deaf to me,
lest, if you be silent to me,
    I become like those who go down to the pit.
2 Hear the voice of my pleas for mercy,
    when I cry to you for help,
when I lift up my hands
    toward your most holy sanctuary.
3 Do not drag me off with the wicked,
    with the workers of evil,
who speak peace with their neighbors
    while evil is in their hearts.
4 Give to them according to their work
    and according to the evil of their deeds;
give to them according to the work of their hands;
    render them their due reward.
5 Because they do not regard the works of the LORD
    or the work of his hands,
he will tear them down and build them up no more.
6 Blessed be the LORD!
    For he has heard the voice of my pleas for mercy.

7 The LORD is my strength and my shield;
   in him my heart trusts, and I am helped;
my heart exults,
   and with my song I give thanks to him.
8 The LORD is the strength of his people;
   he is the saving refuge of his anointed.
9 Oh, save your people and bless your heritage!
   Be their shepherd and carry them forever.

Day 29: Is it His Will?

You ask and do not receive, because you ask amiss, that you may spend it on your pleasures. James 4:3

Sometimes God says "no" to our prayers because our requests don't line up with His will. And sometimes we ask for things that God knows would not be good for us.

James is addressing people that are not yielding their will to God. They aren't thinking about God's plan or what is best, they are asking for things that will only bring self-gratification.

They are living their own way. Verse 2 describes the people he's addressing as people who *lust and do not have. You murder and covet and cannot obtain.*

God is not a genie here to give us a certain number of wishes. He is not at our mercy. He will not answer our prayers if we jump through certain hoops, do things right, or "earn" the right to have our prayers heard.

Our God is the ultimate authority. He has a perfect plan and a perspective that we lack. We can't convince the Lord of our requests; we must align our prayers with His will. This is why Jesus says in the Lord's prayer, our model prayer:

Your kingdom come. Your will be done on earth as it is in heaven. Matthew 6:10

Examine your intentions. When you pray are you attempting to convince God to satisfy your own pleasures, or are you aligning yourself with the heart of God?

Prayer:
Dear Lord, Your kingdom come. Your will be done on earth as it is in heaven. My desire is to have your plan succeed. I want to pray for your plans and your passions, Lord. Give me the ability to see past my own selfish desires to see the bigger picture. Don't give me the things I ask for that will hurt me or my relationship with you. Thank you for saying 'no' to me when my prayers are amiss. In Jesus name, Amen.

Continue writing your prayer here:

Day 29: Is it His Will?

1. Has God ever said no to a selfish prayer of yours?

2. How will you focus on God's plan instead of your own?

3. What makes it difficult to accept a "no" answer from God?

Day 29: JOURNAL

Take a few moments to stop and LISTEN to the Lord; then write down what you sense He is telling you. Is He giving you words of encouragement and support for yourself that you should note? Is He asking you to encourage or support someone in particular? Is He showing you an adjustment you need to make in your life? Have you seen answered prayers? Write these things down so you create a record of God's goodness to you.

Day 30

Waiting Patiently

Pray: "Lord, I'm afraid to pray for patience but I want to wait patiently for You. Thanks for hearing me."

Scripture: Psalm 40 – Excerpts

I waited patiently for the Lord; he inclined to me and heard my cry. ² He drew me up from the pit of destruction, out of the miry bog, and set my feet upon a rock, making my steps secure.
³ He put a new song in my mouth, a song of praise to our God.
Many will see and fear, and put their trust in the Lord.
⁴ Blessed is the man who makes the Lord his trust, who does not turn to the proud, to those who go astray after a lie! ⁵   You have multiplied, O Lord my God, your wondrous deeds and your thoughts toward us; none can compare with you! I will proclaim and tell of them, yet they are more than can be told.
⁶ I sacrifice and offering you have not delighted, but you have given me an open ear. Burnt offering and sin offering you have not required. ⁷ Then I said, "Behold, I have come; in the scroll of the book it is written of me: ⁸ I delight to do your will, O my God; your law is within my heart." ⁹ I have told the glad news of deliverance in the great congregation; behold, I have not restrained my lips, as you know, O Lord. I have not hidden your deliverance within

my heart; I have spoken of your faithfulness and your salvation; I have not concealed your steadfast love and your faithfulness from the great congregation. ¹¹ As for you, O Lord, you will not restrain your mercy from me; your steadfast love and your faithfulness will ever preserve me! ...

¹⁶ But may all who seek you rejoice and be glad in you; may those who love your salvation say continually, "Great is the Lord!" ¹⁷ As for me, I am poor and needy, but the Lord takes thought for me.

You are my help and my deliverer; do not delay, O my God!

Day 30: Waiting Patiently

Therefore be patient, brethren, until the coming of the Lord. See how the farmer waits for the precious fruit of the earth, waiting patiently for it until it receives the early and latter rain. You also be patient, establish your hearts, for the coming of the Lord is at hand. James 5:7,8

James reminds his readers that just because something is not happening right now does not mean that God won't accomplish His plan. He will fulfill prophecy and bring justice, making wrong things right again.

We don't always see what's happening behind the scenes. While James' readers were getting frustrated that Jesus hadn't returned, he reminds them that God is still at work, even if it's not the timing they had pictured.

The disciples were frustrated when Jesus wasn't taking the throne and establishing political freedom. They had an idea of what being set free looked like, and He wasn't what they pictured. Jesus was the Messiah; He was what they had prayed for. God simply had a bigger plan for salvation that wasn't limited to the type of freedom His people expected.

Are you limited in the way you expect God to answer your prayers? Are you ever anxious and frustrated that things aren't happening in your timing the way that you pictured? Slow down and read James 5:7-8 again.

Prayer:
Father, thank you for your timing. Thank you for looking deeper to my core needs. Please give me patience in
_____.
(Situation that comes to mind).
May my faith be built by being patient and establishing my heart in you. In Jesus name, Amen.

Continue writing your prayer here:

Day 30: Waiting Patiently

1. Has God ever surprised you with the way He's answered a prayer? When?

2. Read James 5:7-8 again. What should your response be when you haven't seen God answer yet?

3. What makes being patient and waiting for God to answer prayer difficult?

Day 30: JOURNAL

Take a few moments to stop and LISTEN to the Lord; then write down what you sense He is telling you. Is He giving you words of encouragement and support for yourself that you should note? Is He asking you to encourage or support someone in particular? Is He showing you an adjustment you need to make in your life? Have you seen answered prayers? Write these things down so you create a record of God's goodness to you.

Day 31

Testing Your Faith

Pray: "Lord, thank you that you are enough."

Scripture: Philippians 3:1-16

Finally, my brothers, rejoice in the Lord. To write the same things to you is no trouble to me and is safe for you.

² Look out for the dogs, look out for the evildoers, look out for those who mutilate the flesh. ³ For we are the circumcision, who worship by the Spirit of God and glory in Christ Jesus and put no confidence in the flesh— ⁴ though I myself have reason for confidence in the flesh also. If anyone else thinks he has reason for confidence in the flesh, I have more: ⁵ circumcised on the eighth day, of the people of Israel, of the tribe of Benjamin, a Hebrew of Hebrews; as to the law, a Pharisee; ⁶ as to zeal, a persecutor of the church; as to righteousness under the law, blameless. ⁷ But whatever gain I had, I counted as loss for the sake of Christ. ⁸ Indeed, I count everything as loss because of the surpassing worth of knowing Christ Jesus my Lord. For his sake I have suffered the loss of all things and count them as rubbish, in order that I may gain Christ ⁹ and be found in him, not having a righteousness of my own that comes from the law, but that which comes through faith in Christ, the righteousness from God that depends on faith— ¹⁰ that I may know him and the power of his resurrection, and may share his sufferings, becoming like him in his

death, ¹¹ that by any means possible I may attain the resurrection from the dead.

¹² Not that I have already obtained this or am already perfect, but I press on to make it my own, because Christ Jesus has made me his own. ¹³ Brothers, I do not consider that I have made it my own. But one thing I do: forgetting what lies behind and straining forward to what lies ahead, ¹⁴ I press on toward the goal for the prize of the upward call of God in Christ Jesus. ¹⁵ Let those of us who are mature think this way, and if in anything you think otherwise, God will reveal that also to you. ¹⁶ Only let us hold true to what we have attained.

Day 31: Testing Your Faith

God said no to Paul. Paul asked the Lord to remove 'a thorn in the flesh'. He asked him three times. The first two times it appeared as though God didn't answer at all and then the third time, he plead with him; God's answer was that Paul had to instead lean on Him.

Concerning this thing I pleaded with the Lord three times that it might depart from me. And He said to me, "My grace is sufficient for you, for My strength is made perfect in weakness." Therefore, most gladly I will rather boast in my infirmities, that the power of Christ may rest upon me. 2 Corinthians 12:8,9

Sometimes God says no because by denying our request, we have the opportunity to grow closer to Christ. Our dependency on Him might not be as deep if He answers our request the way we want. His desire for a relationship with us, for the strengthening of our faith, will sometimes come before our comfort.

Paul's response to God is not to complain. He recognizes that God has something higher to attain through his weakness. *Therefore I take pleasure in infirmities, in reproaches, in needs, in persecutions, in distresses, for Christ's sake. For when I am weak, then I am strong. 2 Corinthians 12:10*

Also Read: Philippians 3:8-10 to see how Paul's faith is secured, how willing he is to cling to Christ above all else.

Prayer:

Dear Lord, I know that your grace is sufficient for me, and your strength is made perfect in my weakness. Thank you for everything You use to grow my faith. I know that when I am weak, I am strong in You. Lord, show me how You want me to respond when you say, "no." Let Your answers, whatever they might be, grow my faith in You and my confidence that You know best. Thank you that You actually care more for me than I am able to care for myself. I trust You with answering every time in ways that are meant for my good and Your glory. In Jesus name, Amen.

Continue writing your prayer here:

Day 31: Testing Your Faith

1. How do you respond when God says no?

2. Recall a time that God has said no to a request. How has He grown your faith in the midst of it?

3. Have you ever had a time in your life where you could or should thank God for unanswered or "no" to your prayers? When?

Day 31: JOURNAL

Take a few moments to stop and LISTEN to the Lord; then write down what you sense He is telling you. Is He giving you words of encouragement and support for yourself that you should note? Is He asking you to encourage or support someone in particular? Is He showing you an adjustment you need to make in your life? Have you seen answered prayers? Write these things down so you create a record of God's goodness to you.

Day 32

The Big Picture

Pray: "Lord, thanks that You know the end when I don't."

Scripture: Philemon - Excerpts

Paul, a prisoner for Christ Jesus, and Timothy our brother,

To Philemon our beloved fellow worker... ⁴ I thank my God always when I remember you in my prayers, ⁵ because I hear of your love and of the faith that you have toward the Lord Jesus and for all the saints, ⁶ and I pray that the sharing of your faith may become effective for the full knowledge of every good thing that is in us for the sake of Christ. ⁷ For I have derived much joy and comfort from your love, my brother, because the hearts of the saints have been refreshed through you. ⁸ Accordingly, though I am bold enough in Christ to command you to do what is required, ⁹ yet for love's sake I prefer to appeal to you—I, Paul, an old man and now a prisoner also for Christ Jesus— ¹⁰ I appeal to you for my child, Onesimus, whose father I became in my imprisonment. ¹¹ (Formerly he was useless to you, but now he is indeed useful to you and to me.) ¹² I am sending him back to you, sending my very heart. ¹³ I would have been glad to keep him with me, in order that he might serve me on your behalf during my imprisonment for the gospel, ¹⁴ but I preferred to do nothing without your consent in order that your goodness might not be by compulsion but of your own accord. ¹⁵ For this perhaps is why he was parted from you for a while, that you might have him back forever, [16] no longer as a bondservant but more than a bondservant, as a beloved brother—especially to me, but how much more to you, both in the flesh and in the Lord. [17] So if you consider me your partner, receive him as you would receive me. [18] If he has wronged you at all, or owes you anything, charge that to my account. [19] I, Paul, write this with my own hand: I will repay it—to say nothing of your owing me even your own self. [20] Yes, brother, I want some benefit from you in the Lord. Refresh my heart in Christ. [21] Confident of your obedience, I write to you, knowing that you will do even more than I say. [22] At the same time, prepare a guest room for me, for I am hoping that through your prayers I will be graciously given to you. ..[25] The grace of the Lord Jesus Christ be with your spirit.

Day 32: The Big Picture

God moves in ways we don't expect. Neither Philemon, Paul or Onesimus could have anticipated or expected God to move in the way He did. He knows the big picture when we only have a glimpse.

Come now you who say, "Today or tomorrow we will go to such and such a city, spend a year there, buy and sell, and make a profit; whereas you do not know what will happen tomorrow. For what is your life? It is even a vapor that appears for a little time and then vanishes away. Instead, you ought to say, "If the Lord wills, we shall live and do this or that." James 4:13-15

Even with good intentions, we can't always anticipate what God is going to do or how He is going to answer our prayers. Our ideas are limited. Even if they are good ideas, God might have something different and better.

In Acts 16:6-10 we see that Paul tries repeatedly to go in the direction he believes God is leading. His intentions were great; to preach the gospel and do God's work. But God had in mind very specifically that Paul was to go to Macedonia. Verse 7 says that *after they had come to Mysia, they tried to go into Bithynia, but the Spirit did not permit them*. Then a vision appeared to Paul and God gave him clarity as to what He was doing.

If God is saying no to you, ask Him to make clear what His yes is. You might feel frustrated as your plans fail but allow God to show you where He is directing you. He may have something better and more significant for you around the corner. If there doesn't seem to be an answer wait and ask God to give you the peace to wait until He is ready to show you where your next step should be.

Prayer:

Thank you Lord for seeing what I don't! Stop me when I boast about tomorrow and instead remind me that if you will, I will do this or that. Help me accept your 'no', having faith that you know what is best and it will be accomplished.

Talk to the Lord specifically about anything that you need the bigger picture perspective in.

Continue writing your prayer here:

Day 32: The Big Picture

1. Have you ever had God say "no" to something only to discover something better was in store?

2. What are you praying for now that you need God's 'bigger picture' perspective in?

Day 32: JOURNAL

Take a few moments to stop and LISTEN to the Lord; then write down what you sense He is telling you. Is He giving you words of encouragement and support for yourself that you should note? Is He asking you to encourage or support someone in particular? Is He showing you an adjustment you need to make in your life? Have you seen answered prayers? Write these things down so you create a record of God's goodness to you.

Day 33

Is Anything In Between?

Pray: "Lord, let me be real with You, like you are with me."

Scripture: Malachi 3:6-18

"For I the LORD do not change; therefore you, O children of Jacob, are not consumed. ⁷ From the days of your fathers you have turned aside from my statutes and have not kept them. Return to me, and I will return to you, says the LORD of hosts. But you say, 'How shall we return?' ⁸ Will man rob God? Yet you are robbing me. But you say, 'How have we robbed you?' In your tithes and contributions. ⁹ You are cursed with a curse, for you are robbing me, the whole nation of you. ¹⁰ Bring the full tithe into the storehouse, that there may be food in my house. And thereby put me to the test, says the LORD of hosts, if I will not open the windows of heaven for you and pour down for you a blessing until there is no more need. ¹¹ I will rebuke the devourer for you, so that it will not destroy the fruits of your soil, and your vine in the field shall not fail to bear, says the LORD of hosts. ¹² Then all nations will call you blessed, for you will be a land of delight, says the LORD of hosts.

¹³ "Your words have been hard against me, says the LORD. But you say, 'How have we spoken against you?' ¹⁴ You have said, 'It is vain to serve God. What is the profit of our keeping his charge or of walking as in mourning before the LORD of hosts? ¹⁵ And now we call the arrogant blessed.

Evildoers not only prosper but they put God to the test and they escape.'"

¹⁶ Then those who feared the LORD spoke with one another. The LORD paid attention and heard them, and a book of remembrance was written before him of those who feared the LORD and esteemed his name. ¹⁷ "They shall be mine, says the LORD of hosts, in the day when I make up my treasured possession, and I will spare them as a man spares his son who serves him. ¹⁸ Then once more you shall see the distinction between the righteous and the wicked, between one who serves God and one who does not serve him.

Day 33: Is Anything In Between?

Sometimes God doesn't answer our prayers because our sin is in the way of our relationship with Him. As Isaiah explains, God is capable of answering; of saving us and hearing our cries. But our sins cause our relationship to be broken. It can't be made right until we go to Him for forgiveness. Then He can once again hear us and answer our cries.

Behold, the Lord's hand is not shortened, that it cannot save; nor His ear heavy, that it cannot hear. But your iniquities have separated you from your God; and your sins have hidden His face from you, so that He will not hear. For your hands are defiled with blood, and your fingers with iniquity; your lips have spoken lies, your tongue has muttered perversity. Isaiah 59:1-3

The Old Testament is full of instances where the Israelites decided to go their own way and God in turn withheld blessing and answers to their prayers.

Sow for yourselves righteousness; reap in mercy; break up your fallow ground, for it is time to seek the Lord, till He comes and rains righteousness on you. Hosea 10:12

The Lord is willing and wanting to have a right relationship with you. He wants to answer you, He wants to have communication with you. Take the step to seek the Lord. He wants to hear from you and is delighted when you sincerely ask Him to make your heart right with Him.

Prayer:
Dear God, please forgive me for_____.
I don't want anything to come between my relationship with you. Please keep me aware of my sins that I might confess continually and make things right with you. I know I can't be good enough on my own so thank You that in Your grace and mercy all my sins are already covered. I confess them because I don't want them to get in the way of our relationship or of You hearing my prayers. Please hear me and answer me. In Jesus name, Amen.

Continue writing your prayer here:

Day 33: Is Anything In Between?

1. Ask the Lord to reveal anything coming in between your relationship with Him. What comes to mind?

2. What can you do now to 'sow for yourself righteousness and reap in mercy'?

Day 33: JOURNAL

Take a few moments to stop and LISTEN to the Lord; then write down what you sense He is telling you. Is He giving you words of encouragement and support for yourself that you should note? Is He asking you to encourage or support someone in particular? Is He showing you an adjustment you need to make in your life? Have you seen answered prayers? Write these things down so you create a record of God's goodness to you.

Day 34

...Yet I Will Rejoice

Pray: "Lord, let me see You so clearly through my troubles that I can praise You no matter what happens."

Scripture: Habakkuk 3 – Excerpts

A prayer of Habakkuk the prophet, according to Shigionoth.

2 O Lord, I have heard the report of you, and your
    work, O Lord, do I fear. In the midst of the
    years revive it; in the midst of the years make it
    known; in wrath remember mercy.

3 God came from Teman, and the Holy One from
    Mount Paran.
His splendor covered the heavens,
    and the earth was full of his praise.

4 His brightness was like the light;
    rays flashed from his hand;
    and there he veiled his power.

5 Before him went pestilence,
    and plague followed at his heels....

16 I hear, and my body trembles;
    my lips quiver at the sound;
rottenness enters into my bones;
    my legs tremble beneath me.
Yet I will quietly wait for the day of trouble
    to come upon people who invade us.

17 Though the fig tree should not blossom,
    nor fruit be on the vines,
  the produce of the olive fail
    and the fields yield no food,
  the flock be cut off from the fold
    and there be no herd in the stalls,
18 yet I will rejoice in the LORD;
    I will take joy in the God of my salvation.
19 GOD, the Lord, is my strength;
    he makes my feet like the deer's;
    he makes me tread on my high places.

Day 34: ...Yet I Will Rejoice

Habakkuk got sick of God saying no. He was seeing horrible things happen and wasn't seeing God answer his prayers. This is what he says in his anguish.

O Lord, how long shall I cry, and you will not hear? Even cry out to You, "Violence!" and You will not save. Why do You show me iniquity, and cause me to see trouble? For plundering and violence are before me; there is strife, and contention arises. Therefore the law is powerless, and justice never goes forth. For the wicked surround the righteous; therefore perverse judgment proceeds. Habakkuk 1:2-4

Habakkuk was honest with God and waited expectantly for God to answer. He didn't understand why God wasn't giving relief and shared with God his perspective. God answers.

Look among the nations and watch- be utterly astounded! For I will work a work in your days which you would not believe, though it were told you. Habakkuk 1:5

God understands Habakkuk's frustration and He answers his heart when he cries out. God tells him that it's not over and He has a plan, even when it looks like things are spinning out of control. Habakkuk felt like God was saying no and that He was absent from the events taking place, when in actuality God's hand was orchestrating events and getting ready for something astounding.

Even when it doesn't feel like it or seem like it, God is still in control. Ask Him and He'll show you how.

Prayer:
Father, thank you for hearing me. Thank you for working a work in my days. Open my eyes to what you are doing, that I would recognize and rejoice in the creative way you answer my prayers and orchestrate everything to bring glory to Yourself.
Today, ask God your questions, sharing your heart honestly, and expect His answer.

Continue writing your prayer here:

Day 34: ...Yet I Will Rejoice

1. How hard is it for you to be honest with God in prayer, even when it isn't pretty?

2. What can we learn from Habakkuk's conclusion?

3. What events in your life might feel like they are spinning out of control, and you need affirmation that God's hand is still in charge?

Day 34: JOURNAL

Take a few moments to stop and LISTEN to the Lord; then write down what you sense He is telling you. Is He giving you words of encouragement and support for yourself that you should note? Is He asking you to encourage or support someone in particular? Is He showing you an adjustment you need to make in your life? Have you seen answered prayers? Write these things down so you create a record of God's goodness to you.

Day 35

Getting Better Results

Pray: "Lord, thanks that you hear me and deliver me!"

Scripture: Psalm 34 – Excerpts

I will bless the LORD at all times;
 his praise shall continually be in my mouth.
2 My soul makes its boast in the LORD;
 let the humble hear and be glad.
3 Oh, magnify the LORD with me,
 and let us exalt his name together!
4 I sought the LORD, and he answered me
 and delivered me from all my fears.
5 Those who look to him are radiant,
 and their faces shall never be ashamed.
6 This poor man cried, and the LORD heard him
 and saved him out of all his troubles.
7 The angel of the LORD encamps
 around those who fear him, and delivers them.
8 Oh, taste and see that the LORD is good!
 Blessed is the man who takes refuge in him!
9 Oh, fear the LORD, you his saints,
 for those who fear him have no lack! …
15 The eyes of the LORD are toward the righteous
 and his ears toward their cry.
16 The face of the LORD is against those who do evil,
 to cut off the memory of them from the earth.

17 When the righteous cry for help, the LORD hears
  and delivers them out of all their troubles.
18 The LORD is near to the brokenhearted
  and saves the crushed in spirit.
19 Many are the afflictions of the righteous,
  but the LORD delivers him out of them all.
20 He keeps all his bones; not one of them is broken.
21 Affliction will slay the wicked,
  and those who hate the righteous will be
    condemned.
22 The LORD redeems the life of his servants;
  none of those who take refuge in him will be
    condemned.

Day 35: Getting Better Results

There are times when our lives get turned upside down and we don't know what to do with ourselves. Psalm 34 lets us know that there is no time when we should not be praising God. His praises should be continually in our mouths. There are times when that is much easier said than done. I've been afraid for my life and needed to remember and pray:

"I sought the LORD, and he answered me and delivered me from all my fears. Vs. 4

There was a time when I lost everything financially. I was bankrupt and embarrassed about it. And then I remember the response we should have to that:

This poor man cried, and the Lord heard him and saved him out of all his trouble.

That does not mean the finances will necessarily be restored. Believe it or not, God's picture of what is best for us now and eternally is more important than the size of our checking, savings, or investment account. He loves us too much to give us too much.

The Psalmist tells us the Lord hears the righteous when they call for help. It's helpful here to remember that the only way we are righteous is because Jesus paid the price for us. But because He did, we are, and we are seen that way. This has nothing to do with how good we are but everything to do with who we are in Him. He even warns us that the righteous will have problems:

Many are the afflictions of the righteous, but the LORD delivers him out of them all.

Isn't God's honesty refreshing! It's another reason for us to take our refuge (safety) in Him. When we do, He promises us that we will not be condemned. What a good God!

Prayer:
Lord, thank you that you love it when we reach out to You. I'm praying today to see the results of You in my life in tangible ways; ways that will have me praising You and telling others about how great You are and how You answer my prayers. In Jesus name, Amen.

Continue writing your prayer here:

Day 35: Getting Better Results

Look over the last six days of devotions

1. What new things have you learned about God and prayer?

2. How has this week affected your prayer life?

3. What have you learned or prayed about that you can practically apply to your life?

Day 35: JOURNAL

Take a few moments to stop and LISTEN to the Lord; then write down what you sense He is telling you. Is He giving you words of encouragement and support for yourself that you should note? Is He asking you to encourage or support someone in particular? Is He showing you an adjustment you need to make in your life? Have you seen answered prayers? Write these things down so you create a record of God's goodness to you.

Day 36

Persistence Pays

Pray: "Lord, strengthen me so that I can persist in my prayers."

Scripture: Luke 18:1-8

And he told them a parable to the effect that they ought always to pray and not lose heart. [2] He said, "In a certain city there was a judge who neither feared God nor respected man. [3] And there was a widow in that city who kept coming to him and saying, 'Give me justice against my adversary.' [4] For a while he refused, but afterward he said to himself, 'Though I neither fear God nor respect man, [5] yet because this widow keeps bothering me, I will give her justice, so that she will not beat me down by her continual coming.' " [6] And the Lord said, "Hear what the unrighteous judge says. [7] And will not God give justice to his elect, who cry to him day and night? [z] Will he delay long over them? [8] I tell you, he will give justice to them speedily. Nevertheless, when the Son of Man comes, will he find faith on earth?"

Mark 13:5-13

And Jesus began to say to them, "See that no one leads you astray. [6] Many will come in my name, saying, 'I am he!' and they will lead many astray. [7] And when you hear of wars and rumors of wars, do not be alarmed. This must take place, but the end is not yet. [8] For nation will rise against nation, and kingdom against kingdom. There will be earthquakes in various places; there will be famines. These are but the beginning of the birth pains.

⁹ "But be on your guard. For they will deliver you over to councils, and you will be beaten in synagogues, and you will stand before governors and kings for my sake, to bear witness before them. ¹⁰ And the gospel must first be proclaimed to all nations. ¹¹ And when they bring you to trial and deliver you over, do not be anxious beforehand what you are to say, but say whatever is given you in that hour, for it is not you who speak, but the Holy Spirit. ¹² And brother will deliver brother over to death, and the father his child, and children will rise against parents and have them put to death. ¹³ And you will be hated by all for my name's sake. But the one who endures to the end will be saved.

Day 36: Persistence Pays

Ask and it will be given to you; seek and you will find; knock, and it will be opened to you. For everyone who asks receives and he who seeks finds, and to him who knocks it will be opened. Matthew 7:7-8

The Greek words 'ask, seek and knock' in these verses are in the present tense meaning continued petition; not a quick one-time prayer followed by an instant answer. Jesus is urging us to be consistent and persistent in our requests. Dogged tenacious determination is something God appreciates even to the point of what might seem annoying to some. God loves a passionate and persistent heart and wants us to seek Him that way.

And let us not grow weary while doing good, for in due season we shall reap if we do not lose heart. Galatians 6:9

God honors a diligent seeker. He loves to answer us. He doesn't ask us to be persistent because it takes a lot to convince him of our case. He asks us to be persistent because through it we gain understanding of the character of God, our relationship with Him deepens, and it is evidence that we are serious about seeking His face. Patient endurance is a quality trait God appreciates in His children. And it's a trait we can work on developing. For some of us this will be harder than others, but the benefits are terrific.

We live in a culture that expects immediacy. We want fast internet, speedy cars, food as we drive through, and public policy that provides instant results. A relationship with the Living God is not built by a fast prayer on the go, five-minute devotionals before bed, and an efficient Sunday worship service. Let the Spirit of God permeate everything you do. Keep an attitude of prayer and worship all day. Be persistent and do not weary of doing good!

Prayer:
God, change my ideas about needing things fast and efficiently. Slow me down so that I can gain understanding of you, so that my relationship with you can deepen. Put on my heart things that you want me to be praying for persistently. Remind me of yourself in my daily routine so that I can keep an attitude of prayer and worship. In Jesus name, Amen.

Continue writing your prayer here:

Day 36: Persistence Pays

1. What is something you have prayed diligently about? What came of it?

2. What is something you should be praying persistently about?

3. When you expect things to come fast and easy and they don't, how does that affect your relationship with God?

Day 36: JOURNAL

Take a few moments to stop and LISTEN to the Lord; then write down what you sense He is telling you. Is He giving you words of encouragement and support for yourself that you should note? Is He asking you to encourage or support someone in particular? Is He showing you an adjustment you need to make in your life? Have you seen answered prayers? Write these things down so you create a record of God's goodness to you.

Day 37

All Occasions

Pray: "Lord, help me to find a reason to pray in everything."

Scripture: Matthew 6:10-18

"Beware of practicing your righteousness before other people in order to be seen by them, for then you will have no reward from your Father who is in heaven. ² "Thus, when you give to the needy, sound no trumpet before you, as the hypocrites do in the synagogues and in the streets, that they may be praised by others. Truly, I say to you, they have received their reward. ³ But when you give to the needy, do not let your left hand know what your right hand is doing, ⁴ so that your giving may be in secret. And your Father who sees in secret will reward you.
⁵ "And when you pray, you must not be like the hypocrites. For they love to stand and pray in the synagogues and at the street corners, that they may be seen by others. Truly, I say to you, they have received their reward. ⁶ But when you pray, go into your room and shut the door and pray to your Father who is in secret. And your Father who sees in secret will reward you.
⁷ "And when you pray, do not heap up empty phrases as the Gentiles do, for they think that they will be heard for their many words. ⁸ Do not be like them, for your Father knows what you need before you ask him. ⁹ Pray then like this:

"Our Father in heaven, hallowed be your name. Your kingdom come, your will be done, on earth as it is in heaven. Give us this day our daily bread, and forgive us our debts, as we also have forgiven our debtors. And lead us not into temptation, but deliver us from evil. [14] For if you forgive others their trespasses, your heavenly Father will also forgive you, [15] but if you do not forgive others their trespasses, neither will your Father forgive your trespasses. [16] "And when you fast, do not look gloomy like the hypocrites, for they disfigure their faces that their fasting may be seen by others. Truly, I say to you, they have received their reward. [17] But when you fast, anoint your head and wash your face, [18] that your fasting may not be seen by others but by your Father who is in secret. And your Father who sees in secret will reward you.

Day 37: All Occasions

So Jesus answered and said to them, "Have faith in God. For assuredly, I say to you, whoever says to this mountain, 'Be removed and be cast into the sea,' and does not doubt in his heart, but believes that those things he says will be done, he will have whatever he says. "Therefore I say to you, whatever things you ask when you pray, believe that you receive them and you will have them. Mark 11:22-24

Nothing is too small or big to bring to God in prayer. God often puts specific things in our mind that we are passionate about so that we can pray our passions.

Pray on all occasions. Don't limit your talks with God to a designated devotional time. Pray whenever something comes to your attention. Pray before your feet hit the ground in the morning, pray during mealtime, pray in your car, or pray for God's preparation before an event or meeting.

Be comprehensive in what you pray about. Don't get in a rut praying the same blessing over meals, or just for sicknesses. Pray for salvations for people in your life. Pray for your neighbors, your pastor, your family. Pray for opportunities to share Christ. Pray Scripture over your children. Praying for people other than yourself helps you keep your focus outward toward others and upward toward God, and that's good!

Praying comprehensively is something you can practice as a family. Keep a list of prayer requests so you can watch as God answers. Post reminders of things you would like to pray for.

Prayer:

Lord, help me think outside of the box. I want to be a good steward of things you give me to pray for. Starting today I want to pray on this occasion _____. _____and I want to pray comprehensively by praying about _____.
Lord, help me to keep my mental arrows pointed out in prayer. Show me who you want me to pray for and show me how to do that. In Jesus' name, Amen.

Continue writing your prayer here:

Day 37: All Occasions

1. What do you feel compelled to pray about, something God has put on your heart?

2. What occasions in your day can you use to pray?

3. How has God answered your prayers this past week?

Day 37: JOURNAL

Take a few moments to stop and LISTEN to the Lord; then write down what you sense He is telling you. Is He giving you words of encouragement and support for yourself that you should note? Is He asking you to encourage or support someone in particular? Is He showing you an adjustment you need to make in your life? Have you seen answered prayers? Write these things down so you create a record of God's goodness to you.

Day 38

Staying Aligned

Pray: "Lord, help to stay humble, seek Your face and pray!"

Scripture: 2 Chronicles 7:11-22

Thus Solomon finished the house of the LORD and the king's house. All that Solomon had planned to do in the house of the LORD and in his own house he successfully accomplished. [12] Then the LORD appeared to Solomon in the night and said to him: "I have heard your prayer and have chosen this place for myself as a house of sacrifice. [13] When I shut up the heavens so that there is no rain, or command the locust to devour the land, or send pestilence among my people, [14] if my people who are called by my name humble themselves, and pray and seek my face and turn from their wicked ways, then I will hear from heaven and will forgive their sin and heal their land. [15] Now my eyes will be open and my ears attentive to the prayer that is made in this place. [16] For now I have chosen and consecrated this house that my name may be there forever. My eyes and my heart will be there for all time. [17] And as for you, if you will walk before me as David your father walked, doing according to all that I have commanded you and keeping my statutes and my rules, [18] then I will establish your royal throne, as I covenanted with David your father, saying, 'You shall not lack a man to rule Israel.'

[19] "But if you turn aside and forsake my statutes and my commandments that I have set before you, and go and serve other gods and worship them, [20] then I will pluck you up from my land that I have given you, and this house that I have consecrated for my name, I will cast out of my sight, and I will make it a proverb and a byword among all peoples. [21] And at this house, which was exalted, everyone passing by will be astonished and say, 'Why has the Lord done thus to this land and to this house?' [22] Then they will say, 'Because they abandoned the Lord, the God of their fathers who brought them out of the land of Egypt, and laid hold on other gods and worshiped them and served them. Therefore he has brought all this disaster on them.' "

Day 38: Staying Aligned

Then you will call upon Me and go and pray to Me, and I will listen to you. And you will seek Me and find Me, when you search for Me with all your heart. I will be found by you, says the Lord, and I will bring you back from your captivity; I will gather you from all the nations and from all the places where I have driven you, says the Lord, and I will bring you to the place from which I cause you to be carried away captive. Jeremiah 29:12-14

Have you ever seen someone that always seems to get answers for their prayers? It seems like they are in favor with God and they get results that other people can't seem to get. You think, *I just need them to pray. They must have a direct line to God that I don't* or *they are His favorite.* In actuality, they simply know the heart of God and know how to pray according to it. They spend time seeking God with all their heart.

These verses in Jeremiah are very clear about how we establish good communication with God. We need to be properly aligned with His heart. The first thing this verse says is to call on the Lord. When we call on Him and pray to Him, He says He will listen. When we seek Him with all our heart, He will be found.

To be aligned with the Lord we should be intense about our search. Don't let your search be over! Continue seeking and pursuing God. You will never know all there is to know so there will always be more things to discover. What a joyful and fulfilling process!

Prayer:
Lord, Today I call on you and pray to you. If there are things in me that are not appropriately aligned with You, will You show them to me so that I can correct it and seek you with fervency and expectation that you will be found. I recognize that you are so vast, so deep, that there will always be a pursuit and discovery in our relationship. Thank you, Lord, for being a God that will be found and will listen. In Jesus name, Amen.

Continue writing your prayer here:

Day 38: Staying Aligned

1. What will you do today to be aligned with God in prayer?

2. What will your pursuit of God look like this week?

3. What areas in your life could be better aligned with God?

Day 38: JOURNAL

Take a few moments to stop and LISTEN to the Lord; then write down what you sense He is telling you. Is He giving you words of encouragement and support for yourself that you should note? Is He asking you to encourage or support someone in particular? Is He showing you an adjustment you need to make in your life? Have you seen answered prayers? Write these things down so you create a record of God's goodness to you.

Day 39

Being Proactive

Pray: "Lord, help me keep on the whole armor so I stand for You."

Scripture: Ephesians 6:1-19

Children, obey your parents in the Lord, for this is right. ² "Honor your father and mother" (this is the first commandment with a promise), ³ "that it may go well with you and that you may live long in the land." ⁴ Fathers, do not provoke your children to anger, but bring them up in the discipline and instruction of the Lord.

⁵ Bondservants, obey your earthly masters with fear and trembling, with a sincere heart, as you would Christ, ⁶ not by the way of eye-service, as people-pleasers, but as bondservants of Christ, doing the will of God from the heart, ⁷ rendering service with a good will as to the Lord and not to man, ⁸ knowing that whatever good anyone does, this he will receive back from the Lord, whether he is a bondservant or is free. ⁹ Masters, do the same to them, and stop your threatening, knowing that he who is both their Master and yours is in heaven, and that there is no partiality with him. ¹⁰ Finally, be strong in the Lord and in the strength of his might. ¹¹ Put on the whole armor of God, that you may be able to stand against the schemes of the devil. ¹² For we do not wrestle against flesh and blood, but against the rulers, against the authorities, against the cosmic powers

over this present darkness, against the spiritual forces of evil in the heavenly places. [13] Therefore take up the whole armor of God, that you may be able to withstand in the evil day, and having done all, to stand firm. [14] Stand therefore, having fastened on the belt of truth, and having put on the breastplate of righteousness, [15] and, as shoes for your feet, having put on the readiness given by the gospel of peace. [16] In all circumstances take up the shield of faith, with which you can extinguish all the flaming darts of the evil one; [17] and take the helmet of salvation, and the sword of the Spirit, which is the word of God, [18] praying at all times in the Spirit, with all prayer and supplication. To that end, keep alert with all perseverance, making supplication for all the saints, [19] and also for me, that words may be given to me in opening my mouth boldly to proclaim the mystery of the gospel...

Day 39: Being Proactive

We do not wrestle against flesh and blood, but against principalities, against powers, against the rulers of the darkness of this age, against spiritual hosts of wickedness in the heavenly places. Therefore, take up the whole armor of God, that you may be able to withstand in the evil day, and having done all, to stand. Eph. 6:12

We have a reason to be proactive in our praying. A real battle is waging, and we aren't bystanders, whether we want to be or not. We can't run from this battle; we are in it regardless of our personal desires. So, if you are in it, you might as well win it! Prayer is the most effective weapon we have.

Have you ever seen a situation and said dejectedly, "Well, I suppose all there is left to do is to pray"? Or heard someone else say, "I wish there was something we could do! But I guess we can't do anything...we can only pray."

These statements imply that prayer is less effective than doing something. We feel like prayer is something to do when our hands are tied, and we've run out of options. That is wrong!

Prayer should be our first response and often, our only response. It is the only thing that is guaranteed effective. In Zechariah 4:6 God says: *"Not by might nor by power, but by My Spirit"*. The Spirit of God is what takes action. If He calls us to do something, it will be after prayer and by the power of His Spirit. And there is no more powerful Spirit to be in relationship with.

The real battle is a spiritual battle. And it's a battle where we want to line up on God's side because He WILL be victorious. It's important to make the distinction that we are on God's side, not that we insist He be on our side. Our side should be His side!

Prayer:

Lord, I am sorry for ever thinking prayer is less effective than what I can do. I am sorry for underestimating your power. Please forgive me for having a self-centered perspective. Give me wisdom to know when you are calling me only to prayer. May my actions only be done by the power of your Holy Spirit. In Jesus name, Amen.

Continue writing your prayer here:

Day 39: Being Proactive

1. Is prayer your first or last response to crisis or spiritual battle? Why?

2. In what life situation do you need to take a step back and pray instead of taking your own actions?

3. How can you make sure you are on God's side as opposed to insisting that God be on your side?

Day 39: JOURNAL

Take a few moments to stop and LISTEN to the Lord; then write down what you sense He is telling you. Is He giving you words of encouragement and support for yourself that you should note? Is He asking you to encourage or support someone in particular? Is He showing you an adjustment you need to make in your life? Have you seen answered prayers? Write these things down so you create a record of God's goodness to you.

Day 40

Staying Alert

Pray: "Lord, strengthen me so I can watch and pray for You."

Scripture: Luke 21:29-36

And he told them a parable: "Look at the fig tree, and all the trees. 30 As soon as they come out in leaf, you see for yourselves and know that the summer is already near. 31 So also, when you see these things taking place, you know that the kingdom of God is near. 32 Truly, I say to you, this generation will not pass away until all has taken place. 33 Heaven and earth will pass away, but my words will not pass away.

34 "But watch yourselves lest your hearts be weighed down with dissipation and drunkenness and cares of this life, and that day come upon you suddenly like a trap. 35 For it will come upon all who dwell on the face of the whole earth. 36 But stay awake at all times, praying that you may have strength to escape all these things that are going to take place, and to stand before the Son of Man."

Scripture: 1 Thessalonians 5:1-11

Now concerning the times and the seasons, brothers, you have no need to have anything written to you. 2 For you yourselves are fully aware that the day of the Lord will come like a thief in the night. 3 While people are saying, "There is peace and security," then sudden destruction will come upon them as labor pains come upon a pregnant woman, and they will not escape. ⁴But you are not in darkness, brothers, for that day to surprise you like a thief. ⁵For you are all children of light, children of the day. We are not of the night or of the darkness. ⁶So then let us not sleep, as others do, but let us keep awake and be sober. ⁷For those who sleep, sleep at night, and those who get drunk, are drunk at night. ⁸But since we belong to the day, let us be sober, having put on the breastplate of faith and love, and for a helmet the hope of salvation. ⁹For God has not destined us for wrath, but to obtain salvation through our Lord Jesus Christ, ¹⁰who died for us so that whether we are awake or asleep we might live with him. ¹¹Therefore encourage one another and build one another up, just as you are doing.

Day 40: Staying Alert

Watch and pray, lest you enter into temptation. The spirit indeed is willing, but the flesh is weak. Matthew 26:41

Jesus gets frustrated with His disciples because they don't see the necessity in prayer. They are tired and worn out. They can't see what's coming up so they lose a sense of urgency. Jesus tells them to pray three times and each time He comes back to find them sleeping. As a result, they were not as prepared as they should have been for Jesus' arrest.

Jesus knew that a real battle was waging and that it was to be fought through prayer.

Now in the morning, having risen a long while before daylight, He went out and departed to a solitary place; and there He prayed. Mark 1:35

And when He had sent them away, He departed to the mountain to pray. Mark 6:46

Jesus is the Son of God! If anyone should know the heart of God without asking, it's Jesus. But Jesus is a man of action, and He knows where the action is; in prayer. He knew that to be proactive and prepared, He had to be aligned with the Father and he took the time to make certain that He was.

If Jesus Himself needed to be in constant prayer, how much more must we? If Jesus thought it was that important for him, how much more should it be for us?

Prayer:
Lord, I'm sorry for not staying alert in times you have called upon me. Please forgive me for valuing_____ above prayer. Thank you for showing me through Christ the importance of watching and praying. Show me how to pray and what to pray for. In Jesus name, Amen.

Continue writing your prayer here:

Day 40: Staying Alert

1. Why did the disciples value sleep instead of prayer?

2. What have you been valuing above prayer?

3. How will you change so you can stay alert and watchful?

Day 40: JOURNAL

Take a few moments to stop and LISTEN to the Lord; then write down what you sense He is telling you. Is He giving you words of encouragement and support for yourself that you should note? Is He asking you to encourage or support someone in particular? Is He showing you an adjustment you need to make in your life? Have you seen answered prayers? Write these things down so you create a record of God's goodness to you.

Day 41

Bonus Day - One
United in Prayer

Pray: "Lord, let me be united in my prayer and praise."

Scripture: Acts 2:32-47

This Jesus God raised up, and of that we all are witnesses. ³³ Being therefore exalted at the right hand of God, and having received from the Father the promise of the Holy Spirit, he has poured out this that you yourselves are seeing and hearing. ³⁴ For David did not ascend into the heavens, but he himself says, " 'The Lord said to my Lord, "Sit at my right hand, until I make your enemies your footstool." ' ³⁶ Let all the house of Israel therefore know for certain that God has made him both Lord and Christ, this Jesus whom you crucified." ³⁷ Now when they heard this they were cut to the heart, and said to Peter and the rest of the apostles, "Brothers, what shall we do?" ³⁸ And Peter said to them, "Repent and be baptized every one of you in the name of Jesus Christ for the forgiveness of your sins, and you will receive the gift of the Holy Spirit. ³⁹ For the promise is for you and for your children and for all who are far off, everyone whom the Lord our God calls to himself." ⁴⁰ And with many other words he bore witness and continued to exhort them, saying, "Save yourselves from this crooked generation." ⁴¹ So those who received his word were baptized, and there were added that day about three thousand souls.

⁴² And they devoted themselves to the apostles' teaching and the fellowship, to the breaking of bread and the prayers. ⁴³ And awe came upon every soul, and many wonders and signs were being done through the apostles. ⁴⁴ And all who believed were together and had all things in common. ⁴⁵ And they were selling their possessions and belongings and distributing the proceeds to all, as any had need. ⁴⁶ And day by day, attending the temple together and breaking bread in their homes, they received their food with glad and generous hearts, ⁴⁷ praising God and having favor with all the people. And the Lord added to their number day by day those who were being saved.

Bonus Day: United in Prayer

And they devoted themselves to the apostles' teaching and the fellowship, to the breaking of bread and the prayers. [43] And awe came upon every soul, and many wonders and signs were being done through the apostles. [44] And all who believed were together and had all things in common.

These disciples, these people that created the Church, were not just getting together for a Sunday worship service. These verses don't describe an hour to hear from the Lord, praise Him a little and give something, before going separate ways. This was far more significant, intimate, and relational. And prayer with each other is a main ingredient of the purpose for which they were gathering.

These people were spending many meals together and welcoming each other into their homes to pray, to talk about what God was doing and to encourage each other's journey with Christ. They gave all they had, valuing each other over their own needs. They didn't hold back for fear that they might be taken advantage of. I'm certain it happened. But the price was worth being part of what God was doing. It should be the same for us.

What results came from this attitude of unselfish love, constant companionship, and deep accountability? *And the Lord added to the church daily those who were being saved. Acts 2:47*

Community, love, and fellowship like this can exist. It is attainable and it's what the body of Christ should be about. It does take work. Commit yourself to it. People who live this way have more joy, get to see God working in miraculous ways and are more fulfilled. But it means a commitment to a lifestyle of investing in others at your own expense.

Prayer:
Dear God, thank you for creating us with a need for others and the ability to be stronger with others. Help me reach out and respond when others reach out. Break down any defenses in me, that I can be approachable and loving. Give me your eyes to see through and allow me to love others like you love both them and me. In Jesus name I pray, Amen.

Continue writing your prayer here:

Bonus Day - One: United in Prayer

1. What are the benefits of being in a life-giving group?

2. What are you doing to be part of a group that lives like the early church, which is the body of Christ and to whom He is the head?

3. Why do you think God allows for more results when we are united than when we are trying to "go it alone?"

Bonus Day - One: JOURNAL

Take a few moments to stop and LISTEN to the Lord; then write down what you sense He is telling you. Is He giving you words of encouragement and support for yourself that you should note? Is He asking you to encourage or support someone in particular? Is He showing you an adjustment you need to make in your life? Have you seen answered prayers? Write these things down so you create a record of God's goodness to you.

Day 42

Bonus Day - Two:
Don't Give Up

Pray: "Lord make me steadfast for you and thankful."

Colossians 3:1-17

If then you have been raised with Christ, seek the things that are above, where Christ is, seated at the right hand of God. ² Set your minds on things that are above, not on things that are on earth. ³ For you have died, and your life is hidden with Christ in God. ⁴ When Christ who is your life appears, then you also will appear with him in glory.

⁵ Put to death therefore what is earthly in you: sexual immorality, impurity, passion, evil desire, and covetousness, which is idolatry. ⁶ On account of these the wrath of God is coming. ⁷ In these you too once walked, when you were living in them. ⁸ But now you must put them all away: anger, wrath, malice, slander, and obscene talk from your mouth. ⁹ Do not lie to one another, seeing that you have put off the old self with its practices ¹⁰ and have put on the new self, which is being renewed in knowledge after the image of its creator. ¹¹ Here there is not Greek and Jew, circumcised and uncircumcised, barbarian, Scythian, slave, free; but Christ is all, and in all.

¹² Put on then, as God's chosen ones, holy and beloved, compassionate hearts, kindness, humility, meekness, and patience, ¹³ bearing with one another and, if one has a

complaint against another, forgiving each other; as the Lord has forgiven you, so you also must forgive. [14] And above all these put on love, which binds everything together in perfect harmony. [15] And let the peace of Christ rule in your hearts, to which indeed you were called in one body. And be thankful. [16] Let the word of Christ dwell in you richly, teaching and admonishing one another in all wisdom, singing psalms and hymns and spiritual songs, with thankfulness in your hearts to God. [17] And whatever you do, in word or deed, do everything in the name of the Lord Jesus, giving thanks to God the Father through him.

Colossians 4:2-3a

[2] Continue steadfastly in prayer, being watchful in it with thanksgiving. [3] At the same time, pray also for us, that God may open to us a door for the word, to declare the mystery of Christ...

Bonus Day – Two: Don't Give Up

To "continue steadfastly in prayer," means to stick with it, to keep on keeping on. There is something about not giving up that God appreciates in His children. Just like we appreciate it in our children, even if, at times, it can be annoying!

Often as we begin prayer, attacks from our enemy, the devil, intensify. We battle discouragement and distraction before we can even start to be consistent. Should our response be frustration? Fear? Giving up? No! Our response should be to fight back until the enemy flees.

Harder attacks should result in harder prayer. Stay after it, stay on it, let God and anyone else know that you are not going to give up on coming to God. When you dig in and keep at it, He will let you get to know him better and better.

The greatest value in persistent and consistent prayer is not in getting what we have been praying for or getting our prayers answered at all. The greatest value in prayer is to get to know our Savior, Lord, and King better and better. And when we include others in the process, we all benefit from it.

In Acts 12:5 it says that *Peter was therefore kept in prison, but constant prayer was offered to God for him by the church*. His church didn't just pray once. They gathered and gave constant prayer until an angel came, broke his chains, and released him. They got even more than they expected as they persisted.

Prayer:

Dear Lord, give me discernment in knowing how to battle and continue in prayer even when discouragement plagues me. I don't want to give up and I don't want to be oblivious to what's going on around me. Thank You that "no weapon formed against me," by our enemy can stand as I come to You in prayer. Thank You for hearing me and demonstrating again and again that You are a Loving, Caring, Personal God. In Jesus name, Amen.

Continue writing your prayer here:

Bonus Day - Two: Don't Give Up

1. When have you experienced doubt and frustration in prayer?

2. What should your response be?

3. How can you be alerted to recognize when you need persistence?

Bonus Day - Two: JOURNAL

Take a few moments to stop and LISTEN to the Lord; then write down what you sense He is telling you. Is He giving you words of encouragement and support for yourself that you should note? Is He asking you to encourage or support someone in particular? Is He showing you an adjustment you need to make in your life? Have you seen answered prayers? Write these things down so you create a record of God's goodness to you.

The Key is Prayer

CONGRATULATIONS!! If you are reading this and that means you have completed the 40 days plus, then you deserve a hearty congratulations! But you aren't done! The purpose of The Prayer Adventure was only to get you started in praying more effectively and efficiently.

It doesn't matter what your profession is or if you don't have one. Prayer is the key to doing whatever you do in a way that keeps God in the center of it. And when God is in the center of our lives He brings more joy, more peace, and more success. Talking to Him every day and throughout the day will bring each day alive like no other way.

Prayer is the key that separates meetings from divine appointments. Prayer is the key that separates good ideas from God ideas. Prayer is the key that makes the impossible possible. Prayer is the key that takes the best we can do and makes it the best God can do. Prayer is the key that changes our brainstorming to prayer storming. Prayer is the key to seeing God in places where you couldn't see before.

Now it's time to decide if you want to do The Prayer Adventure again, perhaps with some other people, or if you would like to do something different. But keep praying!

By now you should be ready to start writing your own devotionals and letting God show you things in His word that will be life changing, challenging, and growing. I'd like to help get you started with a simple method that has helped me immensely in studying God's word and then praying through what He shows me.

Perhaps you've already heard of the SOAPS method of studying the Bible. I've added the last "S" to the traditional model. It's an acronym for: Scripture, Observation, Application, Prayer, and Share. It works simply and once you catch on you and God become the author of your devotions. And that's a great place to be.

S O A P S
BIBLE STUDY METHOD

BEGIN: Start by preparing to pray. That means minimize distractions so you can focus. Then ask God to speak to you by the power of the Holy Spirit as you open His word and begin to read. Ask the Holy Spirit to "highlight," or make a part of what you read jump out at you so that you will know what He would like to speak to you today through His word.

S: SCRIPTURE: What scripture stuck out to you the most? Write it down and read it out loud.

O: OBSERVATION: What do you observe in general about the scripture you have written? What do you think God is saying? Is there a promise? Is there a call to action or honor? Is there a truth that God is announcing? Who is it for? Who wrote it and to whom is it addressed? (Don't feel the need to answer all the questions. Go where the Spirit leads)

A: APPLICATION: How does this scripture, promises and/or truth apply to your life? Does it call you to make adjustments in how you are living? Is it giving you an assignment to carry out? Is confession, forgiveness, prayer, or praise warranted or called for because of what you've read? How does God want it to make a difference for you?

P: PRAYER: Write out a prayer describing how to implement what you have learned and what God is showing you. Pray for others that God brings to your mind. Praise God for His blessings and opening your eyes to His truth and promises.

S: SHARE: Share what God has shown you with someone else sometime today. This will give God the glory, imprint it on your mind and give testimony to God's goodness.

S.O.A.P.S.
Bible Study Method - Example

Scripture: Colossians 1:1-14

1 Paul, an apostle of Christ Jesus by the will of God, and Timothy our brother,
² To the saints and faithful brothers in Christ at Colossae:
Grace to you and peace from God our Father.
³ We always thank God, the Father of our Lord Jesus Christ, when we pray for you, ⁴ since we heard of your faith in Christ Jesus and of the love that you have for all the saints, ⁵ because of the hope laid up for you in heaven. Of this you have heard before in the word of the truth, the gospel, ⁶ which has come to you, as indeed in the whole world it is bearing fruit and increasing—as it also does among you, since the day you heard it and understood the grace of God in truth, ⁷ just as you learned it from Epaphras our beloved fellow servant. He is a faithful minister of Christ on your behalf ⁸ and has made known to us your love in the Spirit.

<u>⁹ And so, from the day we heard, we have not ceased to pray for you, asking that you may be filled with the knowledge of his will in all spiritual wisdom and understanding, ¹⁰ so as to walk in a manner worthy of the Lord, fully pleasing to him: bearing fruit in every good work and increasing in the knowledge of God;</u>
¹¹ being strengthened with all power, according to his glorious might, for all endurance and patience with joy; ¹² giving thanks to the Father, who has qualified

you to share in the inheritance of the saints in light. ¹³ He has delivered us from the domain of darkness and transferred us to the kingdom of his beloved Son, ¹⁴ in whom we have redemption, the forgiveness of sins.

S.O.A.P.S.
Bible Study Method - Example

S: SCRIPTURE: Colossians 1:9-10 [9] And so, from the day we heard, we have not ceased to pray for you, asking that you may be filled with the knowledge of his will in all spiritual wisdom and understanding, [10] so as to walk in a manner worthy of the Lord, fully pleasing to him: bearing fruit in every good work and increasing in the knowledge of God...

O: OBSERVATION: The apostle Paul wants us to know that to understand God's will for us requires spiritual wisdom and understanding. And we will need those things if we want to produce fruit for God's kingdom and carry out His will for us.

A: APPLICATION: To acquire spiritual wisdom and understanding or discern what God's will for me is, I must spend time getting to know God and His character and I will need the Holy Spirit to teach me. It's a lifestyle of learning in relationship with Him. It's not just an educational thing.

P: PRAYER: Lord Jesus, I need your Holy Spirit to direct me, guide me and continue to show me how to live. Thank you that you allow me to produce good fruit when I stay connected to you. Thanks that it's not about working at it but it's about being in relationship with you, listening to you and enjoying the amazing grace you have made available to me. Thank for being willing to use me for your glory and my good. Give me any adjustments in me or assignments for me that you would like me to carry out. Make me a blessing today. Amen!

S: SHARE: I'm sharing it with you and I'm praying it over you like the Apostle Paul did his brothers and sisters in Christ.

S.O.A.P.S.
Bible Study Method – Your Turn!

Scripture: 1 John 5:1-15

Everyone who believes that Jesus is the Christ has been born of God, and everyone who loves the Father loves whoever has been born of him. ² By this we know that we love the children of God, when we love God and obey his commandments. ³ For this is the love of God, that we keep his commandments. And his commandments are not burdensome. ⁴ For everyone who has been born of God overcomes the world. And this is the victory that has overcome the world—our faith. ⁵ Who is it that overcomes the world except the one who believes that Jesus is the Son of God?

⁶ This is he who came by water and blood—Jesus Christ; not by the water only but by the water and the blood. And the Spirit is the one who testifies, because the Spirit is the truth. ⁷ For there are three that testify: ⁸ the Spirit and the water and the blood; and these three agree. ⁹ If we receive the testimony of men, the testimony of God is greater, for this is the testimony of God that he has borne concerning his Son. ¹⁰ Whoever believes in the Son of God has the testimony in himself. Whoever does not believe God has made him a liar, because he has not believed in the testimony that God has borne concerning his Son. ¹¹ And this is the testimony, that God gave us eternal life, and this life is in his Son. ¹² Whoever has the Son has life; whoever does not have the Son of God does not have life.

¹³ I write these things to you who believe in the name of the Son of God, that you may know that you have eternal

life. ¹⁴ And this is the confidence that we have toward him, that if we ask anything according to his will, he hears us. ¹⁵ And if we know that he hears us in whatever we ask, we know that we have the requests that we have asked of him.

S.O.A.P.S.
Bible Study Method – Your Turn!

S: SCRIPTURE:

O: OBSERVATION:

A: APPLICATION:

P: PRAYER:

S: SHARE:

A Note from Cliff

Hopefully it's been as great a journey for you as it has been for me. I've been praying that by now the habit is firmly in place and you are changed because of it. If that's happened to you then the truth is, I thanked God in advance for you!

Now take a few moments and reflect on the journey. Ask God to bring to your memory some of the things you've learned along the way and make a note of them.

Go back and look at what you asked for in the beginning of your 40 plus days. Has there been some direct answers to prayer? Can you see that God has been active and working in your life? I want to encourage you to write those things down and to share them with others. It's often in the sharing that God gets the glory He so richly deserves. It's also in the sharing that we so often get blessed for being a blessing.

By the way, if God has spoken to you, shown up in surprising way or miraculously answered your prayers, I would love to hear from you! You can email your story to me at Cliff@cliffnotes.live.

Thank you!

May God bless you and keep you. May He make His face shine upon you and be gracious to you. May He turn His face toward you and give you His peace and strength so that you will bear great fruit for Jesus and continue to grow in the knowledge of Him. And may you overflow with joy giving frequent thanks to our Father in Heaven. In the powerful name of Jesus. Amen!

WE INVITE YOU TO

ORDER BOOKS IN BULK (20+)

REQUEST SMALL GROUP MATERIALS

OR INVITE CLIFF TO SPEAK
FOR YOUR CHURCH OR ORGANIZATION

EMAIL: CLIFF@CLIFFNOTES.LIVE
CALL: 360-333-3661

CONTINUE THE ADVENTURE
WWW.CLIFFNOTES.LIVE